D1515210

PASSCHENDAELE
AND THE BATTLES OF YPRES 1914-18

MARTIN MARIX EVANS

PASSCHENDAELE

AND THE BATTLES OF YPRES 1914-18

OSPREY
MILITARY

Military Editors: Lee Johnson/Sharon van der Merwe
Design: The Black Spot
Cartography by Micromap, courtesy Pitkin Guides

Filmset in Singapore by Pica Ltd.
Printed through World Print Ltd., Hong Kong

For a catalogue of all books published by Osprey Military please write to:
Osprey Marketing, Reed Books, Michelin House,
81 Fulham Road, London SW11 6RB

ACKNOWLEDGEMENTS

The constructive and patient assistance of David Fletcher and his staff of the Tank Museum,
Bovington (TM); Jan Dewilde of the Documentatiecentrum In Flanders Fields, Ypres (IFF); Mark
Berteloot of Provinciale Bibliotheek en Cultuurarchief, St Andries (PBC-Brugge); Dr Tröger of the
Bayerisches Hauptstaatsarchiv, Munich (BH); Marie-Pascale Prévost-Bault of the Historial de la
Grande Guerre, Péronne (HGG); and the staff of the Department of Photographs, Imperial War
Museum, London (IWM) are gratefully acknowledged. Once more a particular debt of gratitude
is owed to Toby Buchan and Dominique Enright for their work on the script.

The illustrations are subject to copyright and the sources are acknowledged using the abbrevia-
tions given above. The modern colour photographs are by the author with the exception of those
marked DP which are by David Playne. Ordnance Survey maps are Crown Copyright.

The quotations from George Ashurst, D.G. Browne, Ernest Parker, E.W. Swinton and the Earl
Percy and Edwin Vaughan are taken from their own books which are listed in the bibliography. The
words of Graham Williams are from *Christmas Truce* by Malcolm Brown and Shirley Seaton, and
those of Jim McPhee from *The ANZACs* by Patsy Adam-Smith. The numerous quotes of other eye-
witnesses are from the works of Lyn Macdonald, *1914 – The Days of Hope, 1915 – The Death of
Innocence* and *They Called it Passchendaele,* which have made such an outstanding contribution to
our knowledge of the First World War. The literary executors of certain authors quoted have not
been traced at the time of going to press and the author will be grateful for any information as
to their identity and whereabouts.

1st and 2nd Ypres

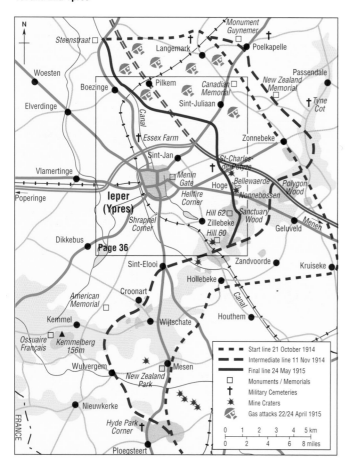

Battle of Messines Ridge and 3rd Ypres

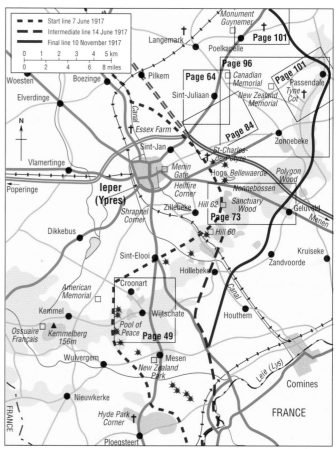

CONTENTS

NOTE ON THE MAPS (Left)

Contemporary Ordnance Survey maps are used to illustrate the British knowledge of the battle front at the time. The grid lines are marked as continuous lines at intervals of 1,000 yards (914 metres) and as dotted lines at half that distance. Each block of 30 squares has an identifying letter, and each square within that block a number. Each square is divided into quarters and reference to these subdivisons is by the notional letter a, b, c, or d, starting top left and reading left to right. References to locations made in the text use this system. Annotations and markings on the maps were made at the time, and some of the maps show signs of wear and tear. The maps associated with the contents list are marked to give the pages on which the particular area is shown in detail. One German map is also included, with 1,000 metre squares.

NOTE ON PLACE NAMES

The convention for place names have altered over the years. Both Flemish and French spellings have been used in books consulted, and the British versions in use during the First World War differ from the modern style. In the text the British spellings have been used, with references to present day Flemish spellings where it may be useful to visitors. Apologies are offered for any inadvertent failure to adhere to this style. The maps associated with the contents list use modern Flemish to assist travellers.

Half title page **Troops sheltering in dug–outs. (IFF)**
Title page **Vickers machine–gun crews in hastily dug positions. (IFF)**

THE FORMATION OF THE WESTERN FRONT

Germany had planned for the possibility of war on two fronts and in the summer of 1914 was faced with the reality. The complex of alliances that was intended to stabilise Europe led, with a ghastly inevitability, to war. Austria-Hungary declared war on Serbia, Russia came in to support the Serbs, Germany to support Austria-Hungary and France to support Russia, so that Germany had enemies to the east and to the west. The answer to this had been devised by Colonel-General Count Alfred von Schlieffen, Chief of the German General Staff from 1891 to 1905. A lightning strike was to finish France in a mere six weeks, swinging through the Netherlands and Belgium to envelop Paris, before the Germans turned back eastwards to deal with the Russians. Meanwhile the French, concentrating on their border with the lost lands of Alsace-Lorraine, annexed by Germany after her victory in the Franco-Prussian War of 1870, and confident in the power of such fortifications as those above Verdun, had devised Plan XVII, an attack eastwards from Nancy to regain the territory seized by the Prussians. In the event, Plan XVII failed utterly.

The Schlieffen Plan had been modified by the new CGS, Colonel-General Helmuth von Moltke, to leave out Holland, and assumed that neutral Belgium would either capitulate or offer insignificant resistance. The fact that Belgian neutrality was guaranteed by Great Britain was not taken seriously; after all, the rulers of Germany and Britain were cousins; but then, so too were the rulers of Russia and Germany. The British ultimatum on the matter was due to expire at 11pm on

Main picture **French infantry on the Nieuport-Ypres front in October 1914.** (IFF)

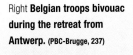

Right **Belgian troops bivouac during the retreat from Antwerp.** (PBC-Brugge, 237)

4 August. Seven hours before the deadline the Germans crossed the border. King Albert of the Belgians had declined to co-operate and the Belgian Army, small – 117,000 men – and ill-equipped though it was, proved to be less of a pushover than expected. The invading troops found themselves attacked by sharpshooters hidden in the hedges and razed the little town of Hervé in revenge. The huge power of the German Army was turned on Liège on 5 August, but the citadel and the twelve forts resisted. Even when the central defence had been taken by a brigade under General Erich Ludendorff the forts held out and had to be subdued one by one over the next ten days after massive artillery pieces had been brought up. The tide of the German progress could not be stopped, but the stubborn resistance it met infuriated the invaders, whose acts of reprisal, such as the burning of the library at Louvain, fuelled the perception throughout the world of "gallant little Belgium" being raped by the "Prussian Beast".

The British Cabinet were shocked to hear that the war might be a long one.

In Britain moves were afoot to send troops across the Channel, but the force available was pathetically small. In Germany military service was compulsory for all men between the ages of 18 and 45. A soldier would first join the 1st Ban of the Landsturm while awaiting call-up at the age of 20, when he would serve for two years (or three in the case of artillery and cavalry) before being transferred to the Reserve where he would remain until he was 28. Five years with the 1st Ban of the Landwehr followed, then another six with the 2nd. The final years were with the 2nd Ban of the Landsturm. Those who were not called up at the age of 20, students and so forth, were placed in an Ersatz Reserve. Germany thus had an army with a peacetime strength of some 840,000 men, and a very substantial number of Reservists.

France also had a system of military service, with men being called up for a three-year period followed by seven years in the Reserve. In accordance with French plans, the greater number of her troops were on the eastern border of the country.

The British Regular Army, on the other hand, was a volunteer force and was largely deployed in the defence and retention of the Empire. As a result the British Expeditionary Force that was conveyed to France between 12 and 22 August numbered only 120,000 men. It was, however, a highly professional organisation. On 6 August the British Cabinet had debated whether they should be sent to France at all and were shocked to hear

Left **Corporal, The Rifle Brigade (Prince Consort's Own). The original BEF wore uniform of the 1908 pattern and its infantrymen were largely equipped with the Mark III .303-inch short magazine Lee-Enfield rifle. The cavalry used a short carbine version.** (Osprey, Warrior 16, *British Tommy*) (Mike Chappell)

Below left **Corporal, 50th Regiment of Infantry, French Army.
The uniform varies little from that of 1870 and is conspicuous
at a considerable distance.** Below right **Zouave, 2nd Regiment
of Zouaves. The winter uniform was adopted for
service in Europe, but was already being
replaced by khaki by November 1914.**
(Osprey, MAA 286, *French Army 1914-1918*)
(Gerry Embleton)

Above **The invasion of Belgium and the brutal German conduct
there, at least as it was reported, gave rise to a wave of
protest in Britain. The Daily Telegraph raised funds for the
relief of Belgian refugees by publishing** *King Albert's Book*,
from which this illustration by Arthur Rackham is taken.
(MFME Nov95/37, Rackham Estate)

the view of Field Marshal Lord Kitchener, the
Secretary of State for War, that the war might be
a long one and that immediate steps must be
taken to raise volunteers. On 7 August the appeal
went out for 100,000 men to enlist and volunteers poured in at the rate of 1,500 a day, but it
would take many months before they could be
trained to a level that made them useful in the
field. This "New Army", as it was called (though it
was almost always referred to as "Kitchener's
Army") received its true baptism of fire in 1916
on the first day of the Battle of the Somme.

The French High Command appeared to be
oblivious to events in Belgium, concentrating as
they were on the execution of Plan XVII. In vain
did General Charles Lanrezac, commanding the
French Fifth Army, report that more than 700,000
Germans were pouring through Belgium and beg

to be allowed to move west to set up a line along the River Sambre. It was not until a detachment of Lanrezac's I Corps had been in action against the Germans at Dinant on 15 August, a fight in which Lieutenant Charles de Gaulle was wounded, that General Joseph Joffre, Commander-in-Chief of the French armies in northern and north-eastern France, issued the order to move the Fifth Army to the Sambre.

On 20 August the Germans entered Brussels and the Belgians fell back on Antwerp. The BEF was on the move towards Mons with the exhortations of their Commander-in-Chief, Field Marshal Sir John French, ringing in their ears, "…we are fighting for right and honour." They were to link with French to their right and advance against the Germans. In the event the pressure of the German advance prevented the formation of a solid line with their allies and, though they gave an excellent account of themselves on 23 August, they had to fall back. Although obliged to divide the force to besiege Antwerp, the right wing of the invading armies thrust south as the great arm of the Schlieffen attack hinged around Luxemburg. By the end of the month they were closing on Paris and, sure of

victory, and persuaded that the BEF had been wiped out at Le Cateau on 26 August, General Alexander von Kluck swung his First Army eastwards, abandoning the envelopment of the French capital. His men had covered more than 200 miles and the lines of supply were terribly overstretched.

General Joffre was now concentrating on the preservation of the French Army and the protection of Paris. His Sixth Army, of which von Kluck was unaware, was concentrating on Paris, the BEF was east of the city and the Fifth Army was to their right. On 4 September General Joseph Gallieni, Commander of the Army of Paris, implored Joffre to authorise an attack on von Kluck's exposed flank. For this British co-operation was vital and, sadly, it took a lot of getting. Joffre agreed with his former chief, Gallieni, on an attack on 6 September, but the BEF was still falling back to the Seine as previously agreed. Joffre copied his orders to the French armies to British headquarters and followed it up with a personal visit, driving some 115 miles to arrive at 2.30pm on 5 September. In an impassioned plea he told French that the honour of England was at stake. Sir John, deeply moved, promised that the British

The prize was control of the Channel ports of Dunkirk, Calais and Boulogne.

Left **German troops heaving a 21cm howitzer into position in front of Antwerp.** (IFF)

Above **General Léonard presents decorations for bravery to French troops at Vincennes.** (MFME Hist/Somme 3.2, HGG)

would do all they possibly could. France's Sixth Army, under General Joseph Maunoury, made first contact with the German First Army on the River Ourcq on the afternoon of 5 September and von Kluck had to turn his force westwards to resist and counter-attack, which he did so successfully that reinforcements to Maunoury's army were transported from Paris by any possible means, including taxis.

The turn opened a gap between the German First and Second Armies into which the BEF all too cautiously advanced, allowing time for the invaders to withdraw, though not without heavy loss, to re establish a coherent line on the Aisne. The Schlieffen Plan had failed in its execution.

On 12 September the Allies launched themselves at the new German defences north of the Aisne. Both BEF and French Fifth Army units managed to cross the river, but the Germans held a dominant position on the heights above the valley and, after six days of fighting, the attack failed. On 14 September von Moltke, a broken man, was in effect replaced as Chief of the German General Staff by General Erich von Falkenhayn. The opposing lines now ran from Compiègne eastwards through Verdun and beyond almost continuously, but to the west there was nothing save the Belgians' gallant resistance in Antwerp. Both sides attempted to exploit the enemy flank.

For the Germans the prize was control of the Channel ports of Dunkirk, Calais and Boulogne through which British supplies could be moved so swiftly, but it was necessary to transfer the German Fourth Army, under Duke Albrecht of Württemberg, from the east to produce the manpower required. On 17 September the French Sixth Army attacked on the Oise, on 22 September their Second Army was in action south of Péronne and on 27 September the line east of Albert, where so many British lives would be lost in the first Battle of the Somme, came into being. Meanwhile the German heavy guns were pounding the Belgians and a small British force in Antwerp, which fell at last on 10 October. The BEF was withdrawn from the Aisne front and sent north – to Ypres.

THE FIRST BATTLE OF YPRES

The town had already seen its fair share of war.

The ancient town of Ypres stands at the southern border of Flanders with flat marshy land stretching away to the north-west, gently rolling fields to the north-east and the hills to the south rising to overlook the area. This has been border country for centuries and the town, a prosperous wool-trading centre in the twelfth century, had already seen its fair share of war by 1800. It was besieged by the English in 1383, taken and fortified by the Burgundians and then seized by the Habsburgs before coming under Spanish rule. The moats and bastions are owed to Vauban under French occupation.

As it became clear that Antwerp could not hold out, Belgian troops and the small British force 8,000 men of the Royal Marines and Royal Naval Division who arrived on 4 and 5 October, retreated. The Belgians and some British went south along the coast, 1,600 British to the Netherlands where, under international law as it applied to neutral countries, they were interned for the duration of the war, some to England, and the rest became prisoners. The French fell back from Ghent on 7 October and the British 7th Division, landed at Zeebrugge the same day and ordered to Bruges, fell back with them. The elements of a new line began to form with King Albert establishing his hold at Nieuport on the coast, where the Ieperlee River and the Canal de l'Yser from Ypres, a continuation of the Ypres-Comines Canal south of the town, runs to join the Yser through Dixmude, then passes though the dyke-drained land and reaches the sea. The situation was very confused. On 3 October a small German detachment was in Ypres, but had to withdraw two weeks later. The British troops transferred from the Aisne regained Bailleul on 14 October, but the Germans secured Lille the day before. Armentières was taken by the British on 18 October, as was Ypres.

Below **The dramatic skyline of the Cloth Hall and Cathedral in Ypres, restored after the war.** (MFME Ypres)

The so-called 'mountains' of Flanders hold Ypres in an embrace.

The so-called "mountains" of Flanders hold Ypres in an embrace from the south-west to the north-east. They are not mountains in any true sense of the word, but in this low-lying terrain even their modest height bestows outstanding advantage upon the army that commands them. They are part of a long, curved, undulating ridge from the Mont des Cats, south-west of Poperinghe, at about 520

Above **Men of the 2nd Scots Guards digging trenches near Zandvoorde under the command of Lieutent E. C. T. Warner, October 1914.** (IWM Q.57231)

Right **British machine-guns coming up into action (left) and a cavalry support entering the grounds of Hollebeke Château, October 1914.** (IWM Q.60752/Paul Maze)

A tenuous line had formed, and from that line the attack to regain Belgium would be mounted.

feet (158 metres) by way of Mont Noir at 410 feet (125m), Mount Kemmel at 520 feet (159m), Wytschaete, at the northern end of the bump known as the Messines Ridge, at 269 feet (82m), Hill 60 at 197 feet (60m, of course), Hill 62 which is six feet higher, and on through Polygon Wood, turning north to Broodseinde and then to Passendale, which the English recall as Passchendaele, at 167 feet (51m). As mountains, not impressive; but from Broodseinde the bulk of Mount Kemmel ten miles away seems almost close enough to touch (see photograph p.97), and the steep sides of the ridge running north to Passchendaele provide not only a

look-out but a defensive position of enviable and daunting strength.

From the ridge the rainwater trickles down to form rivulets and then streams and rivers, all heading north and east for Nieuport. The canal through Ypres forms a significant barrier, but even the apparently puny waterway of the Steenbeek and its tributaries, cutting between Pilckem and Langemarck from Zonnebeke by way of St Julien on its way to join yet other streams, is both a natural trench and a vital drain to wet agricultural land. Indeed, many of these streams receive water from ditches cut to dry the land and without

Right **Belgian front-line positions on the River Ieperlee at Sas; a parapet of sandbags gives cover.**
(PBC-Brugge 228)

Below right **In some places the waterlogged soil made digging trenches impossible. Here, on the Belgian Army's front, sandbags and a wooden firestep make up the defensive position.**
(PBC-Brugge 145)

The airmen overflying the battle reported the movement of huge bodies of German troops behind the lines.

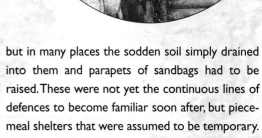

them the earth becomes waterlogged. The earth itself is by no means consistent in its character, varying from sand to clay, and carefully mapped later in the war (see p.100) to show its suitability for dug-outs; and equally its propensity to form mud holes. This is the countryside that was to become known to history as the Ypres Salient.

On 14 October the 7th Division entered Ypres and advanced to hold the ridge to the east across the road to Menin. To their left were the French and beyond them, along the line of the canal and on to the coast, the Belgians. On the right were more French and then British troops on the Messines Ridge. A tenuous line had formed, and from that line the attack to regain Belgium would be mounted. In the meantime trenches were dug for protection against enemy fire where possible,

but in many places the sodden soil simply drained into them and parapets of sandbags had to be raised. These were not yet the continuous lines of defences to become familiar soon after, but piecemeal shelters that were assumed to be temporary.

The planned advance to take Menin on 19 October was known to the Germans, who had captured a British officer carrying his orders. At the same time the German intention to strike for

the Channel ports was on the point of being put into action as Duke Albrecht's Fourth Army moved up into position. The attempt on Menin was repulsed and the airmen overflying the battle reported the movement of huge bodies of German troops behind the lines. The British strength had been increased by the arrival of I Corps under General Sir Douglas Haig, but their numbers were still much less than those of the

Germans they faced. The Fourth Army consisted of XIII, XV, XVI, and II Bavarian Corps. The Allies round Ypres had General Marie Henry de Mitry's Cavalry Corps with French Territorial troops in front of Boesinghe, the British 3rd Cavalry Division facing Poelcapelle, the 7th Division under Major-General Thompson Capper and now reporting to Lieutenant-General Sir Henry Rawlinson, Bt, commander of the partly formed IV

Above **The German Cemetery at Langemarck, where the bodies of the student soldiers killed in the *Kindermord von Iepern* lie buried.** (MFME Ypres)

Left **German uniforms of 1914. Left to right: trooper, 3rd Brandenburg Hussar Regiment; grenadier, 1st Prussian Guard, "Kaiser Alexander Grenadier Regiment"; 2nd lieutenant, 1st Prussian Foot Guards; trooper, 2nd Prussian Guard Machine Gun Detachment.** (Osprey, MAA 80, *German Army 1914-18*) (Gerry Embleton)

King Albert gave the order for the sea-locks at Nieuport to be opened.

Corps, and the 2nd Division of I Corps astride the Menin Road from Zonnebeke to Zandvoorde and Lieutenant-General Edmund Allenby's two divisions of the Cavalry Corps holding the Messines Ridge. The 1st Division was in reserve. They were heavily outnumbered, and, confident that he would witness the breakthrough to the sea, the German Kaiser Wilhelm II took up residence at Thielt, east of Roulers, ready to make a victor's progress into Ypres.

As the attempt against Menin failed the Germans were pressing the exhausted Belgians to the limit and the danger of a collapse of the line from Dixmude to the sea was immediate. That line was also the route of the railway, running high above the dykes and ditches on its embankment and potentially a perfect dam. The road tunnels

beneath it were plugged and, on 21 October, King Albert gave the order for the sea-locks at Nieuport to be opened. During the next four days the flood swiftly spread, up to a mile wide, forming an impassable moat and reducing the Belgian front in the west to a narrow neck of sand and the town of Nieuport itself. With no opportunity of penetrating here, the German Fourth Army hit at the Belgians at Dixmude without success before concentrating its efforts further south; to Ypres.

Also on 21 October, the German attack on the Ypres Salient began. The 7th Division bore the weight of the offensive in the centre while de Mitry's cavalry and the French IX Corps resisted the blow to the north. At Langemarck the Germans threw in their Reserve Corps, student volunteers for the most part, who, full of patriotic enthusiasm and wholly without military training, advanced arm-in-arm, singing. Their losses were terrible, as many as 1,500 dead and 600 taken prisoner, in what became known as the *Kindermord von Iepern*. The rainfall and cold gave a first taste of the foul conditions that were to prevail here for the next four years. By 24 October the fighting had become continuous through day and night and the Germans were penetrating the line. Just north of

1st Grenadier Guards were rushed and the fighting became hand-to-hand with bayonets or with rifles used as clubs.

Gheluvelt on the Menin Road they managed to gain a foothold in Polygon Wood where a battalion of the Royal Warwickshire Regiment held them, swiftly reinforced by the Northumberland Hussars, a Yeomanry reigiment; the Yeomany were the cavalry of the Territorial Force. The fighting amongst the trees was confused and, with no clear line, casualties from "friendly fire" were numerous. The 2nd Battalion Worcestershire Regiment, who were meant to be enjoying time in reserve after the brutal experience of the previous week, were rushed up the Menin Road past Hooge and deployed in the shallow valley (now the route of the motorway) south-west of the wood. Rifle fire was likely to do more harm than good, so they went in with the bayonet, cheering to identify themselves. Captain H. F. Stacke recalled:

The cheer echoed through the wood and was taken up all along the line. The pursuit continued for over half a mile. Then ... sharp bursts of fire from the edge of the open ground brought the advance to a stop. The cheering which had demoralised the enemy's infantry in the wood had also served to warn the German reserves on the far side, and on the edge of the wood the Battalion met a storm of shrapnel and machine-gun bullets. The companies took up the best position they could on the eastern end of the wood and there they dug in.

The wood was now held not by an organised force of identifiable units, but by groups of men from various regiments, huddled in shallow scrapes and clinging on against German pressure. The following day, in autumn sunlight, it became clear that the Germans themselves were in need of respite and the opportunity was taken to relieve the forward troops and not only establish some kind of order in the defence, but prepare to attack.

Above **As the war continued the sophistication of the trenches increased. This French trench in the comparatively dry soil near Loos in 1915 still required revetments and a parapet of sandbags.** (MFME Hist/Somme 1/25. HGG)

Ill-fitting cartridges jammed rifles and two machine-guns became useless

Attack was also the German intention; from 27 to 31 October another six divisions moved into the line facing the Messines Ridge and on 29 October, in thick fog, a massive assault on the flimsy British positions at Gheluvelt began. North of the Menin Road were two companies of the 1st Coldstream Guards and one of the 1st Black Watch (Royal Highlanders), both well below their proper strength, and against them moved three battalions of the 16th Bavarian Reserve Infantry Regiment. They were not seen until they were within 50 yards of the British line. Artillery support for the British was non-existent; restricted by shortage to nine rounds per gun, the available firepower was directed at the enemy batteries. Moreover, the Coldstreamers were hampered by the failure of equipment. Ill-fitting cartridges jammed rifles and two machine-guns became useless for the same reason. The Germans charged and were repulsed, charged again and fell back a second time and doggedly hurled themselves forward a third time to break the thin line of the Black Watch. The Coldstreamers, now fighting on two fronts, not only held on but, with the remnants of the Scots, crushed the intrusion and restored the line. South of the road the 1st Grenadier Guards were rushed in such numbers that the Bavarians managed to turn their left flank and the fighting became hand-to-hand with bayonets or with rifles used as clubs.

The crisis was met with courage and determination by Lieutenant J. A. O. Brooke of the 2nd Gordon Highlanders. He had been sent with a message but, seeing that the line had broken, rallied some 100 men to counter-attack and regain a trench before risking the gunfire to go back for help. His Gordons joined the charge that followed to retake the next trench from which the Bavarians had been laying down heavy fire. The line was secured, some 100 yards to the rear of the morning's position, at the loss of 470 Grenadiers and about 100 Gordon Highlanders. Brooke did not live to see it. He was awarded the Victoria Cross and promoted captain posthumously.

The following day the assault continued, both here and on the Messines Ridge where Allenby's cavalry and the newly arrived French XIV Corps were driven back near Wytschaete. The Bavarian 6th Reserve Division made a determined attack on Gheluvelt, which was almost taken. The German

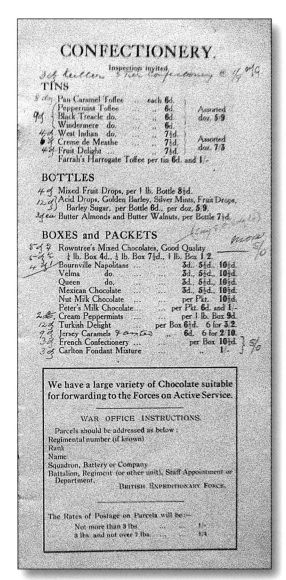

few, the road appeared to be open for the Kaiser's men at last. Shellfire fell on Hooge Château, headquarters of the 1st and 2nd Divisions, killing or wounding all the staff officers. The situation was truly desperate. Haig and French had decided to appeal to the French for help when unexpected good news reached them.

The 2nd Worcesters had been in reserve, if that is how lying up in Polygon Wood could be reasonably described. Brigadier-General Charles Fitzclarence, VC, commanding 1 Guards Brigade, found them there and, realising that here was a chance to plug the gap at Gheluvelt where the South Wales Borderers still clung on round the château, ordered them forward. Shellfire accounted for 100 of them as they rushed towards their objective, but enough survived to turn the tide. The Germans were thrown off the lawns of the great house and the aptly named Lieutenant Slaughter set up a machine-gun to harry their retreat. Private Cole recalled:

They fled in a solid grey mass and we watched the boys winkling them out. Remorseless. It was slaughter. At one point

Above left **The 1914 Christmas catalogue put out by Kingham's Stores offered chocolate, biscuits and other foods for the people of Northampton to send to the troops. The annotations were made during stocktaking.** (Haselwood family archive)

Above **The remains of a concrete bunker still stand today on the tortured summit of Hill 60., so fiercely disputed in 1915 (see p.28).** (DP)

artillery pounded the line and their aircraft dropped the first bombs on Ypres itself. At Zandvoorde the defending Life Guards and a machine-gun detachment of the Royal Horse Guards, fighting dismounted, were wiped out, the Royal Welsh Fusiliers cut to ribbons, and the village was taken, as was Hollebeke. But still the line held.

The artillery resumed its work on Gheluvelt on 31 October with a three-hour bombardment of the shallow trenches. The Royal Field Artillery were forced to pull their guns back as the German infantry massed to attack once more, passing through the remnants of the British troops forced back and digging in for a last stand along the road towards Ypres. Apart from these

in the sunken road we were firing the machine-gun, using dead bodies for cover… We linked up with the Welsh and had to send forward fighting patrols to clear them out of it - and we did it… We plugged the gap to Calais.

The Messines Ridge was also under attack that day. To the north of Wytschaete the French were forced back, though they gave II Bavarian Army Corps a severe mauling near Croonaert Wood (07c, p.49). It was here that Corporal Adolf Hitler won the Iron Cross for rescuing a wounded man under fire. The British clung stubbornly to the ruins of Messines and the pleasant glades of Ploegsteert Wood were shattered by gunfire. The first Territorial infantry regiment to enter the line had their baptism of fire that day and scarcely survived it. The London Regiment was a unit, of many battalions, of the Territorial Force, and strongly affiliated to the Royal Fusiliers (City of London Regiment) of the Regular Army. The 14th London Regiment (London Scottish) had been given the vaguest of orders to act in support of the cavalry holding the ridge and pushed forward through the enemy fire to take their places in the trenches. A third of them fell. In the moonlight of the night that followed they saw shadowy figures advancing and, getting no response to their challenge, opened fire. Private Herbert de Hamel said in his account:

We blazed away into them and I wondered why they lay down in twos and threes to fire back at us. Then suddenly it struck me that they were tumbling over. They made no attempt to rush us, but they still advanced at a steady walk, falling as they came. Flashes spat out along their line… The bullets were cutting through the hedge in front of us and slapped into the bank behind us and all the while, as we tried to fire back, our new rifles jammed and stuck, it might be after one shot or after five shots. You dropped to the bottom of the trench and tugged and banged at the

"It was slaughter. At one point in the sunken road we were firing the machine-gun, using dead bodies for cover…"

Both sides paused. The Germans had already suffered substantial losses and required fresh troops.

bolt to get it free. Then, often as not, it would foul the next cartridge from the magazine and refuse to click home. And all the while the German line was advancing.

That attack failed. The order was given to withdraw, but it did not reach the London Scottish. The next attack engulfed them and only by the chance of smoke from a burning haystack covering their retreat did a handful get away. On Sunday, 1 November, the Germans gained both Wytschaete and Messines but were held from further advance by the courageous resistance of the French 32nd Division and the following day the ridge once more had Allied troops in possession.

Both sides paused. The Germans were surprised by their failure and determined to prevail, but they had already suffered substantial losses and required fresh troops. The Allies were exhausted. The British regiments were reduced to shadows, many of them lacking more than three or four officers and with only a fraction of their men, thus facing operational extinction. On 5 November the 7th Division was withdrawn from the line with only 2,380 men left. The Kaiser was still optimistic, waiting in Menin to strut in triumph. The comparative peace was accompanied by persistent artillery fire, sniping and small raids, affording the defenders of the Salient no rest. On 6 November the British 8th Division landed in France, offering a sliver of hope, but the destruction of Ypres was in progress by shell and incendiary. On 10 November the Germans stormed Dixmude and the next day the battle for Ypres started in earnest once more.

Above **A French sniper,
protected by a metal shield,
looks for a target.** (MFME Hist/
Somme 3/6. HGG)

wood of Nonne Bosschen. Flanking fire fell on them from the 4th Royal Fusiliers (City of London Regiment) on the south of the road and from the 1st Queen's Own Cameron Highlanders on the north as they emerged from the wood. The only other organised formations in the line were about 200 Scots Guards, some men of the Black Watch and of the 2nd Oxfordshire and Buckinghamshire Light Infantry and, at the edge of Polygon Wood, 450 of 1st King's Own (Royal Lancaster Regiment); the rest were gunners, grooms, cooks — anyone capable of holding a rifle. Under their fire the advance stuttered to a halt and the Prussians fell back into the wood. The Oxford and Bucks flushed them out of the wood and fire from the King's took them in the flank; 5 Field Company, Royal Engineers were also in the charge. The cream of the German Army were thrown back, and as the smoke cleared it became evident that the low bank behind which they appeared to have taken cover was a bank of corpses.

Elsewhere the invaders had gained ground. Wytschaete had fallen to them once more and the line in the south now ran from Ploegsteert to Wulvergem, Crooneart and St Eloi. In the north it went from Steenstraat north of Langemarck to swing round to Broodseinde and then west, leaving Gheluvelt in German hands. With a flurry of lesser incidents over the next week the First Battle of Ypres hobbled to a close. The cost had been huge on both sides. British casualties were put at 58,155, including 5,951 men of the Indian Corps, and the French sustained some 50,000 killed and wounded of the 995,000 that 1914 cost them. The Belgians lost 18,522 here, having already suffered over 12,330 casualties out of a total mobilisation of 217,000. The Germans had expended 134,315 with a further 31,265 either missing or made prisoner, nearly a quarter of their total losses of 1914.

For the British the damage done to the BEF was immense, and to the Regular Army irreparable. The peacetime strength at 1 July had been 255,000 men, most of them overseas, which meant that the BEF had, by the end of August, numbered some 120,000 in France and Belgium. The total mobilised that year

The gunfire began at 6.30am, heavier and more concentrated than ever before. The slender line of British and French Zouave troops across the Menin Road, only trivially entrenched, took terrible losses even before the men of the specially assembled Group Linsingen made their move. They were spearheaded by the 1st and 4th Prussian Guards. On the Menin Road the line broke. The battle-weary Zouaves could not stem the flood of Prussians making their way forward from Gheluvelt, along the road and spreading into the

Above **A Minenwerfer, a German mortar, at Hill 60 today.** (DP)

"Christmas trees, adorned with lighted candles, which burnt steadily in the still, frosty air... Then our opponents began to sing Stille Nacht."

was 713,514, so the reservoir of Territorial units had been heavily drawn upon. The losses for 1914 numbered 95,614. Although in August Kitchener's appeal for volunteers had generated a flood of fresh manpower it would be 18 months before they were trained and ready to take the field. Men from the Empire, Australians, Canadians and New Zealanders among them, were on their way and the Indian Army had already sacrificed much, but for the time being at least the British "thin red line" was more a line of perforations. Fortunately, the Germans appeared to be in ignorance of the fact.

With the approach of Christmas the fighting declined and men of both sides did what they could to make their trenches tolerable. The lines of trenches now formed a continuous frontier from the North Sea to Switzerland but at this stage were primitive ditches. In the naturally water-laden soil of Flanders in particular, the trenches acted as drainage ditches and had to be pumped clear of standing water; they could not be made dry. The Army's supply lines became clogged with Christmas mail. In England the newspapers reported that in the six days up to 12 December, the last date for posting, a quarter of a million parcels were sent and the packages that missed the deadline amounted to another 200,000. There were over two and a half million letters.

Attacks on the German lines were still undertaken, mainly to demonstrate to the French that the British support for the cause of ejecting the invader was still strong. On 14 December the 2nd Royal Scots (Lothian Regiment) and the 1st Gordon Highlanders went into action against German positions at Wytschaete after a brief bombardment. They achieved nothing, a few men managing to reach the German line before they fell back. Casualties exceeded 600. Four days later there was a similar fiasco at Ploegsteert Wood.

After the unusually heavy rain of the first three weeks of December, Christmas Eve dawned bright and frosty. The troops on both sides turned their thoughts to the special meals planned to celebrate the next day and even to decorating their miserable living quarters. As evening fell a most curious, and now legendary, thing happened.

As the new year began war returned to the Ypres Salient.

Rifleman Graham Williams of the 1/5th London (London Rifle Brigade) tells of his experience near St Yvon at the north-eastern corner of Ploegsteert Wood.

I was standing on the firestep, gazing towards the German lines and thinking what a very different sort of Christmas Eve this was from any I had experienced in the past... Then suddenly lights began to appear along the German parapet, which were evidently make-shift Christmas trees, adorned with lighted candles, which burnt steadily in the still, frosty air... Then our opponents began to sing Stille Nacht, Heilige Nacht.

The riflemen replied with "The First Nowell" and were rewarded with a rendering of "O Tannenbaum". The exchange continued until both sang together the carol they had in common, "Adeste Fideles". Immediately to the north the 1st Royal Warwickshire Regiment heard the song and the cartoonist Bruce Bairnsfather, the Machine-Gun Officer, saw and heard one of the sergeants swap cigarettes with a German soldier in no man's land. Men of the 2nd Seaforth Higlanders did the same. On Christmas Day the fraternisation continued, the men exchanging cans of food, bottles of drink and tobacco, taking photographs and, as Corporal Robert Renton of the Seaforths reported, burying some of the dead who had been lying between the lines for weeks. The news of this abandonment of enmity shocked and angered the High Commands of both sides and orders were issued forbidding its continuance. As the new year began the temporary truces were ended, often by careful mutual arrangement, and war returned to the Ypres Salient.

THE SECOND BATTLE OF YPRES

By the end of January 1915 the BEF numbered 347,384 men. Many units had been withdrawn from overseas postings in the furthest parts of the British Empire and Territorial regiments had been brought into service. They were organised in two armies. The First Army was under the command of General Sir Douglas Haig and comprised I and IV Corps and the Indian Corps, while General Sir Horace Smith-Dorrien's Second Army was made up of II, III and V Corps. In the Ypres sector the line was held by the Belgians from the coast to Steenstraat, the French from there to the Menin Road and the Second Army on the east and south. The First Army was

The grey expanse is here and there intersected by a road running for some distance.

to their right, from Armentières to La Bassée. The British strength continued to build and the first Canadian troops, commanded by Lieutentant-General Sir Edwin Alderson, entered the line as part of the First Army on 3 March. They played a part on the British left at the Battle of Neuve Chapelle a week later.

On 1 April Haig placed the Canadian Division under the command of Lieutenant-General Sir Herbert Plumer, it thus becoming part of his V Corps. With this increase in manpower the British were now able to take over the front in the Ypres Salient as far north as Poelcapelle, releasing the French IX and XX Corps for use by Joffre elsewhere. Two-thirds of the Salient was now the responsibility of the British.

The Belgian front was described by Lieutenant-Colonel E. W. Swinton and Captain the Earl Percy in their book *A Year Ago*, published in 1916:

In front of the line is a waste of water melting into the sky, and the further bank obscured in mist. The grey expanse is here and there intersected by a road running for some distance on an embankment, and broken by a few trees and hedgerows or the remains of a farm rising up out of the

Right **The memorial to the Canadian troops who withstood the gas attacks of 22-24 April 1915.**

(MFME Ypres 2.4)

flood, on which islands the advanced posts of each side are established. The corpses of long dead German soldiers and the swollen carcasses of cattle and sheep with legs sticking stiffly into the air, drift aimlessly about, while large flocks of wild fowl give the one visible touch of life to the desolate scene. The rifle shots ringing out from the front, the occasional reports of distant guns, and the noise of shells rumbling overhead and bursting with a dull thud far behind, accentuate the prevailing silence.

Nothing could present a stronger contrast to this comparative inaction than the nature of the fighting in progress along the sand dunes farther to the north. Here a desperate struggle at short range continues from day to day, the opposing trenches being situated within a few yards of one another. Here, instead of mud and water, the troops have to endure the wind which blows the sand about in stinging clouds so trying to the eyes as to necessitate the wearing of motor-goggles.

Under the restless drifting sand the configuration of the landscape is continually altering, fresh dunes being formed at one point, while they melt away at another. Perhaps the best description of this area of soft-looking shapeless white mounds is that given by a French officer, who compared it to a land of whipped cream.

Although the Ypres front was, in comparison with the battle of the previous autumn, quiet, the fighting continued in a lower key. Time was found for practical jokes: on 1 April a British airman flew over Lille aerodrome and dropped a football. The German ground crews fled from what appeared to be a new and massive bomb. It rebounded high in the air, and when it finally came to rest was found to carry the message: "April Fool". On 3 April a mine placed at the end of an underground

> ## "In front of the line is a waste of water melting into the sky."

Below **Zouaves, French colonial infantry from Algeria, at Steenstraat, 1915.** (IFF)

Furchtistische Leichen im Schützengraben

working blew up 100 yards of German trench south of the Salient. Sniping was continuous and raids on the enemy by both sides yielded their crop of dead and captured. On 6 April Swinton and Percy noted that prisoners had told of German plans to use poisonous gas to asphyxiate their opponents, but little notice seems to have been taken of this information. Eight days later General Putz, commander of the French Détachement de l'Armée de Belgique, had similar information from a prisoner, Private Jäger of the 234th Reserve Infantry Regiment, taken near Langemarck. So detailed was his account that it was assumed to be an attempt to convey deliberately false intelligence.

The fighting of 1914 had given the Germans an invaluable position from which to overlook all movements around Ypres. Hill 60 (129c, p.36), south of the village of Zillebeke and only a mile and a quarter (2km) from the centre of the town,

gave them a lookout from which the roads running to the south and to the east could be observed with the naked eye. The hill is a man-made feature formed from the spoil dug from the cutting that carries the railway line from Comines. The Germans had taken it from the French in December 1914 and an attempt had been made to take it back in February, without success. Now more complex schemes were to be tried. In early March 1915 171 Tunnelling Company, Royal Engineers, began digging three tunnels for positioning five mines under the hill. The Germans counter-mined. In a new and horrific development of what amounted to medieval siege warfare, camouflets, small explosive charges, were detonated to collapse the other side's workings, burying men alive; sometimes, if a mining party encountered a counter-mining party, hand-to-hand fighting would take place in the bowels of the earth. By 17 April the British explosives were in place and at 7pm that Saturday afternoon they were blown. The German trenches above were shattered and the 150 men in them killed or buried; the very hilltop was blown apart. Instantly the 1st Queen's Own (Royal West Kent Regiment) and the 2nd King's Own Scottish Borderers swept up the hill and, meeting trivial resistance from the 15 dazed survivors, started to dig in. The Germans retaliated at once with shellfire and counter-attacked early on Sunday morning, but were beaten off. The British were reinforced by motor-cycle machine-gun units and the much heavier attack at 7am was also repulsed. All that day and on into the next the struggle continued, the British and Germans each throwing fresh troops into the conflict and each bringing heavier and yet heavier artillery fire to bear upon their opponents. Finally, on 21 April, the fighting eased as the Germans were forced to

At 5pm the Germans opened the valves of 5,730 cylinders of gas.

recognise that the position was lost. By then more than 5,000 dead littered the churned hilltop.

The 1st Canadian Division had taken over the front line south of the Ypres-Poelcapelle road from the French 11th Division between 14 and 17 April. They were not much impressed with the arrangements they inherited. The French, having become used to the strength and vigour of their artillery support, were inclined to man their forward trenches lightly and to withdraw from them when attacked in order to let shellfire destroy the threat. The parapets of the trenches were flimsy, scarce fit to stop a bullet, and there was no parados at all to protect the occupants from shell fragments coming from the rear. Of traverses and communication trenches there were few, if any. The Canadians immediately set about putting matters to rights. The French had also constructed a much more substantial line of defence, termed the GHQ Line, well to the rear, running up from

Zillebeke Lake, west of Hell-Fire Corner, Potijze and Wieltje and turning north-west continuing the line of the modern motorway. As a fall-back position it had its attractions, but, while the front remained further east and north, it merely served to create bottlenecks for troop movements.

To the left of the Canadians were the 45th Algerian Division and beyond them the French 87th Territorial Division, part of General Putz's Groupement d'Elverdinghe. They could not, in fairness, be described as crack troops, but even the bravest would have had difficulty in dealing with what they faced on the afternoon of 22 April. At 5pm the Germans opened the valves of 5,730 cylinders of gas using the soft north-east wind to carry more than 160 tons of chlorine across the French lines. At the least chlorine causes intense irritation of the eyes and breathing difficulty. In greater doses it damages the tissues of the lungs. In extreme cases it causes the lungs to flood with fluid, in effect slowly drowning the victim. No soldier had faced such a weapon before this day. Only the German specialists responsible for its release had any sort of protection against it.

The attack was not part of a strategic plan for a breakthrough to the sea. The Germans themselves were uncertain as to the usefulness of chlorine and this was to some extent an experiment. Moreover, Albrecht's objectives for the Fourth Army were limited by the lack of troops at a time when Germany was making a major effort on the Eastern Front as well. He did hope to drive a wedge between the Belgian and French forces on the western bank of the canal and to occupy that bank far enough to the south to make the Salient untenable, but even these aims were changed during the next few days, becoming more or less ambitious as the situation altered.

Eyes streaming, lungs bursting, those of the the Tirailleurs and the African Light Infantry who could, fled; the rest died. The Canadians watched the cloud of yellow-green gas roll forward over them. The German advance behind the gas was cautious, although well supported by their artillery. In the north, at Steenstraat, they swarmed over the canal bridge and entered Het

The Canadians watched the cloud of yellow-green gas roll forward over them.

Sas, severing contact between the French and the Belgian Grenadiers. Between the Canadians and the canal at Boesinghe there was nothing except the most stubborn of the French, now down by the canal bank. The reaction of the Allies was hasty and necessarily piecemeal.

By 6pm the Germans had occupied Mauser Ridge, running westwards from the plantation named Bois des Cuisiniers (called by the British Kitchener's Wood), but already a new British and French line was in formation composed mostly of Canadian troops with the addition of some 500 Zouaves. Telephone lines were cut by shelling, messages went astray and ignorance and confusion had, for the time, the upper hand. Many of the reports reaching headquarters were quite simply wrong, and led to mistaken decisions. The news started to arrive at General Smith-Dorrien's headquarters at 6.45pm where it was soon appreciated that, to the Canadian left, a gap of some four and a half miles (7.3km) had opened. Alderson and the Canadians were the key to preventing a German breakthrough.

As quickly as possible available units were put at Alderson's disposal; a procedure that was muddled by the difficulty of conveying the orders to the formations themselves and the problems of establishing lines of communication between those units and their temporary commander. Even so, I Canadian Infantry Brigade was released from the Second Army reserve at Vlamertinghe and thus its 2nd and 3rd Battalions, Canadian Infantry, were immediately sent forward. Of the British formations the 2nd East Yorkshire Regiment, the 4th Rifle Brigade, the 2nd Buffs (East Kent Regiment) and the 3rd Duke of Cambridge's Own (Middlesex Regiment) gave Alderson the means to man the ridge north of St Jean as far west as the canal, but a huge gap still existed further forward between Hampshire Farm (C22a, p.36), north of Wieltje, and the canal, with only a lonely French machine-gun nest still in place.

At Steenstraat the release of gas had been incomplete and the resistance the French and Belgians were able to put up was robust. In the centre the Germans had halted, unsure, fortu-nately, of the Allies' position. Further east the initial hesitation of the Germans soon passed, Langemarck was taken by 6pm and the 51st Reserve Division was moving for St Julien. By nightfall Kitchener's Wood had been enveloped and the four British guns there captured. Where the St Julien to Poelcapelle road crosses the stream called the Lekkerboterbeek two platoons of the Canadian 13th Battalion's No.3 Company (3 Brigade, 1st Canadian Division) fought stubbornly until the weight of numbers against them could no longer be resisted. To the south of their position at Vancouver (C6d, p.36) – near the site of the Canadian memorial at Keerselaere on the western tip of the Gravenstafel Ridge – 10 Field Battery, Canadian Field Artillery, enfiladed and halted the Germans making for St Julien before being withdrawn from its exposed position. For

Below **Where the road crosses the former line of Caramel Trench (C16b, see map p.64), a memorial stands to the Canadian attack on Kitchener's Wood, April 1915. The wood no longer exists; it occupied the ground in front of the modern farm building.**
(MFME Yp/Ar 3/13)

We were told to make as much noise as we could and the shouting, swearing, cursing at the tops of our voices was terrific!

his courage in providing cover for this operation machine-gunner Lance-Corporal Frederick Fisher of the 13th Battalion was awarded the VC. He was killed the following day.

True to the French tradition, General Ferdinand Foch, who had been tasked by Joffre with co-ordinating the Allies' operations in the sector, reacted to the situation by proposing counter-attack and the Canadians were asked to act in concert with their allies on their left. Still distracted by the incursion of the Germans at Het Sas and Lizerne, the French were unable to carry out their plan, but the Canadians moved with vigour. At about midnight the 10th and 16th Battalions advanced to "clear wood C.10.d [p.36]"; Kitchener's Wood. What little artillery support they had was concentrated on the northern edge of the wood and soon after the advance had begun heavy fire started to thin the Canadian ranks. They rushed forward, took the trench on the southern side of the wood with the bayonet and hurled themselves forward amongst the trees. Private W. J. McKenna of the 16th Battalion (3 Brigade, 1st Canadian Division) recalled:

… Enemy machine-guns opened about as hot a fire as you could imagine. Men fell in hundreds, but some of us got there, and, when they were facing our bayonets, the Germans were soon beaten and those that weren't killed escaped as fast as they could. We ran through the wood, bayoneting as many as we could catch up with … In order to deceive the enemy in regard to our

numbers, we were told to make as much noise as we could and the shouting, swearing, cursing at the tops of our voices was terrific!

Without the French attack to their left, however, they found themselves with an open flank. They withdrew to the German trench south of the wood and all 500 who were left of the 1,500 who started dug like fury to reverse the defences. The Germans were evidently shaken by Canadian aggression and attempted no new attacks. Meanwhile the 2nd and 3rd Battalions were securing ground south-west of the wood near Oblong and Hampshire Farms, and two companies of the 3rd filled the gap between the edge of the wood and St Julien. The 7th moved to strengthen the Vancouver sector. A line was building.

The other forces available to Smith-Dorrien consisted of small units which were grouped together under temporary command, not an efficient way to organise an army, but there was no alternative. "Geddes's Detachment" was formed of, amongst others, elements of Colonel Geddes's own regiment, the 2nd Buffs, and the 3rd Middlesex Regiment. They were ordered to take position between the Canadian left and the French right. At the same time the 1st and 4th Battalions from 1 Canadian Brigade were sent into almost the same area. It took some time to sort things out. At daybreak they attempted to advance but the 16 guns – eight 18-pounders and eight 4.5-inch howitzers – available to give supporting fire made small impression on the German line on Mauser Ridge and the advance petered out. The French action expected at the same time had again failed to take place as the bulk of reinforcements that Foch could produce were swallowed up in the battle for Steenstraat. Indeed, so vigorous was the German action there that they broke the line between the French and Belgians for a second time that night.

None the less Foch promised Field Marshal French that all the territory yielded by French troops would be regained. As 23 April lengthened into afternoon more British units, many of them

We ran through the wood, bayoneting as many as we could catch up with…

already exhausted in actions further south, below strength and ill-informed of the situation in the north of the Salient, began to arrive to be thrown hurriedly into the line. Part of Geddes's Detachment, the 5th King's Own and the 1st York and Lancaster Regiment, attempted an attack, together with the remnants of 13 Brigade, so badly mauled at Hill 60, astride the Ypres–Pilckem road. They failed again, in part because of becoming confused with the Zouaves and because of lack of co-ordination with their artillery support. But

Julien but still held a line just beyond, near Gravenstafel and the Stroombeek. It was decided by GHQ that a counter-attack should be made to regain the village and General Alderson gave Brigadier-General Sir Charles Hull of 10 Brigade, British 4th Division, command of the patchwork quilt of units allocated to the Canadians. By the morning of 25 April he had been able to contact only half of them but moved, none the less, from the GHQ Line against Kitchener's Wood and St Julien. The 2nd Seaforth Highlanders got to within

A great pall of chlorine rolled down the valley engulfing half the 15th and 8th Battalions

by the end of the day some sort of line had been established to join with the French on the canal.

Duke Albrecht was still determined to take the Salient, and selected the Canadian part of the line north and east of St Julien as his next objective. Here eight battalions, or rather a force approximating that strength made up of diverse units, faced more than three times their number of Germans. At 4am on 24 April the guns began their bombardment and a great pall of chlorine rolled down the shallow valley of the Stroombeek, engulfing half the 15th and 8th Battalions (respectively 3 and 2 Brigades, 1st Canadian Division). The rudimentary cotton face masks with which they had been issued were useless against the gas. From their observation posts in Poelcapelle the Germans controlled artillery fire that systematically plastered the trenches with explosives. Resistance went beyond heroism to a level almost impossible to comprehend, but it could not prevail. Near Keerselaere Lieutenant Edward Bellew of the 7th Battalion (2 Brigade) kept his machine-gun firing until the ammunition was exhausted and then fought on with the bayonet until overpowered. It was not until he was released from a prisoner-of-war camp in 1919 that he learned of his award of the VC. By the end of the day the Canadians had been forced from St

500 yards of the wood while the 1st Princess Victoria's (Royal Irish Fusiliers) and the 2nd Royal Dublin Fusiliers were stopped 200 yards from the village. Seventy-three officers and 2,346 other ranks had fallen, but the gap at St Julien had been plugged. The German force was now turned on the 28th Division's positions at Broodseinde and on the Canadians and the 8th Durham Light Infantry still on the Gravenstafel Ridge. Once more the British had to fall back.

Impressive plans were made to recover ground on 26 April. The French were to attack in force and the Lahore Division, newly arrived to join the Indian Corps, would strike north from St Jean and retake Mauser Ridge. Their fate was the same as that of Geddes's Detachment before them; as soon as they were in sight the German machine-guns cut them down. Major F. A. Robertson of the 59th Scinde Rifles, Frontier Force, reported:

The idea had got about that the German trenches were two hundred yards away. When our front line went over the top they found there was anything from twelve to fifteen hundred yards to go. Our artillery preparation had not at all shaken the nerves of the Germans, and the two

British and four Indian regiments who led the way were absolutely mown down with rifles, machine-guns and artillery of every calibre. The slaughter was cruel. It was men against every machine frightfulness could devise.

The British and Indians still pressed forward, but had to go to ground some 150 yards short of the German line. Then, at 2.20pm, the Germans released gas once more. It engulfed the Lahore Division. The survivors had no choice but to retreat. Their losses were 1,829 men.

Field Marshal French ordered Smith-Dorrien to continue to attack to regain ground, as Foch was telling Putz. Over the next few days more futile operations were mounted with the same ghastly results. With German artillery dominating the Salient as far to the rear as Poperinghe, Smith-Dorrien advocated withdrawing to more stable positions closer to Ypres. In doing so he suggested that the battle was for the ground lost by the French, and that unless they made a real effort to regain it, there was little that could be done. In view of the British losses in the east of the Salient, the comment was scarcely fair, but his overall assessment was entirely realistic. His dispute with his Commander-in-Chief was bitter. On 27 April French ordered Smith-Dorrien to hand over command to General Plumer.

Plans to withdraw, just as Smith-Dorrien had advocated, were immediately formulated by Plumer. Foch protested, but on 1 May Joffre admitted that his priority was the forthcoming action near Arras and therefore additional French reinforcements would not be available. Sir John French was obliged to order Plumer to fall back to a new line.

On the afternoon of 2 May the Germans renewed their use of gas, this time near Mouse Trap Farm (C22b, p.36). The wind did not help them as the fitful breeze dispersed the chlorine and the attack failed. In the calm of the early night of 3 May the 27th and 28th Divisions pulled back to a new line running from Mouse Trap Farm to Frezenberg and thence to the Bellewaarde Ridge

forward of the lake and of Hooge to the eastern edge of Sanctuary Wood. This was achieved without a single casualty. The men of Princess Patricia's Canadian Light Infantry (7 Brigade, 3rd Canadian Division) were not impressed by their new positions on Bellewaarde Ridge, facing Westhoek. There had only been time to dig trenches a couple of feet deep and the rest of the night was occupied with digging deeper and building a parapet of sandbags. With the coming of day German spotter planes found them and dropped flares as markers for their artillery. The shelling and machine-gunning that followed cost the PPCLI 122 men on 4 May, but they held on and consolidated the position.

In spite of their mounting losses, the Germans were still fixed on smashing the Salient. Again gas was used, this time, on 5 May, to spearhead their attack on Hill 60. By nightfall this bloody wilderness was in their hands once more. The heaviest blow fell on 8 May. The artillery bombardment opened on the British trenches at 6am and by the end of the morning the 1st Suffolk Regiment had fallen back from Frezenberg to Verlorenhoek where the motorway crosses the older road today. This left the 2nd Northumberland Fusiliers holding positions east of Mouse Trap Farm north of the break-in and the PPCLI, with the 4th King's Royal Rifle Corps on their right, south of the gap. The Germans attempted to roll up these units on their flanks. Eventually they gained a toe hold on the PPCLI's right and the Canadians had to pull back to the crest of the ridge to fight on. Counter-attacks were going in to prevent any further progress by the Germans at Verlorenhoek and, reinforced by a company of the 4th Rifle Brigade, the PPCLI held on. When relieved at the end of the day they had sustained 392 casualties; there remained 154 of them. But the gap to their north had been closed. The Suffolks had 30 men left. The 3rd Monmouthshire Regiment had 122 and the 12th London Regiment (the Rangers) 54, but by 13 May, when the battle for the Frezenberg Ridge was over, the Germans had still failed to break through.

A small gain cheered 17 May. The French and the Belgian Grenadiers had at last succeeded in

The slaughter was cruel. It was men against every machine.

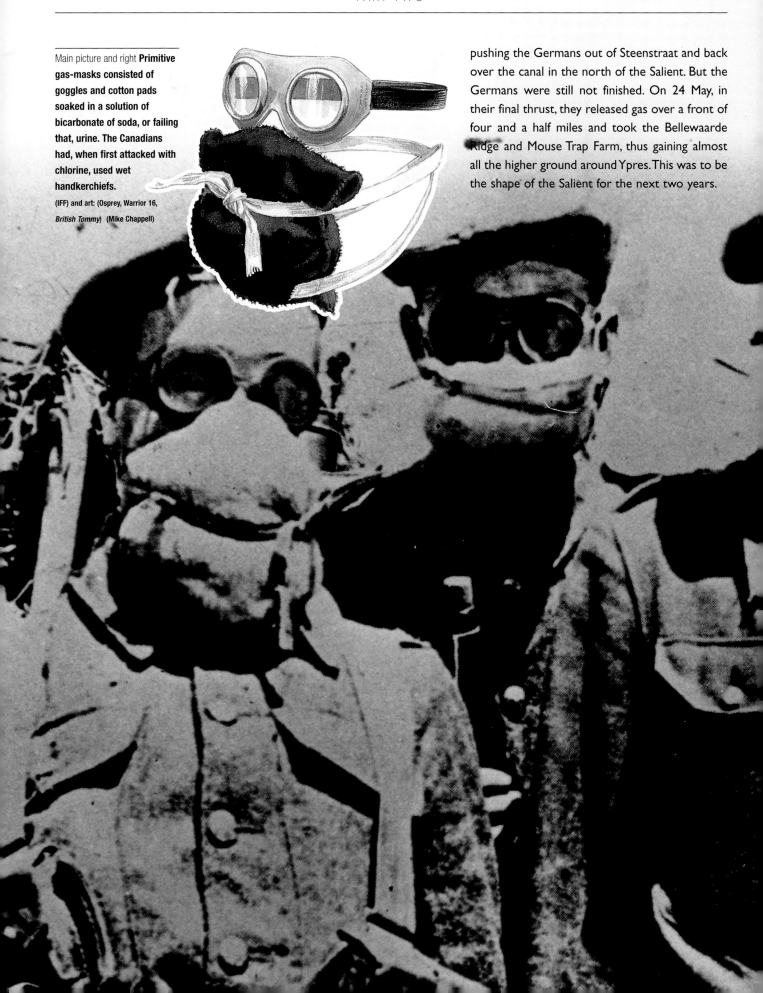

Main picture and right **Primitive gas-masks consisted of goggles and cotton pads soaked in a solution of bicarbonate of soda, or failing that, urine. The Canadians had, when first attacked with chlorine, used wet handkerchiefs.**

(IFF) and art: (Osprey, Warrior 16, *British Tommy*) (Mike Chappell)

pushing the Germans out of Steenstraat and back over the canal in the north of the Salient. But the Germans were still not finished. On 24 May, in their final thrust, they released gas over a front of four and a half miles and took the Bellewaarde Ridge and Mouse Trap Farm, thus gaining almost all the higher ground around Ypres. This was to be the shape of the Salient for the next two years.

In the shattered town itself, which had been mercilessly shelled for a fortnight, the last of the inhabitants were gone. That it was not in German hands was largely the result of the most extraordinary courage of the Canadian and British soldiers and of their allies, and of the resourceful improvisation of their immediate commanders. The BEF suffered 59,275 casualties, of whom 6,341 were Canadian, the French about 10,000 and the Belgians 1,530. German losses totalled 34,933 with a further unknown number of the Marine and XXII Reserve Corps detachments.

Further south, on the Aubers Ridge and at Vimy on 9 May and then at Festubert on 15 May, new attacks held the attention of the generals.

On 24 May, they released gas over a front of four and a half miles.

THE QUIET YEARS

After the intense action of the Second Battle of Ypres the conflict in the Salient continued in a lower key, but to imagine that little took place is a mistake. Swinton and Percy, in their entry for 15 June 1915, stated:

"Last week passed as quietly as it had begun, and of activity on a large scale there is practically nothing to record, the Germans contenting themselves with artillery action against different points and with firing an occasional mine."

The events they do record are two days of shelling of the British line, two mines being

Men were still suffering and dying in terrible circumstances.

exploded by the Germans and the shelling and destruction of a house behind the German lines. The loss of life is not recorded, neither is the agony of enduring an artillery bombardment while huddled in a front-line dugout mentioned and,

Right **French troops prepare a meal within Fort Vaux, one of the massive defensive works above Verdun.** (MFME Hist/Somme 1/33. HGG)

Above **The Germans built solid trenches, intending to hold the ground they had gained. Their troops were, like the Allies, plagued with lice; ridding their clothing of the insects was an enduring preoccupation of the soldiers of both sides.** (IFF)

"…There was a cloud of smoke and dirt five hundred feet high, and an explosion."

straightened the British would be less exposed. The 3rd Division were given the job and on 16 June, after an effective bombardment, took the German front-line trenches without difficulty. The next phase did not go so smoothly as the infantry outran the speed of progress of the artillery barrage. The line was improved, but the ridge was still in German hands, and the British casualties for this small gain came to 3,500 men.

On 19 July Hooge was again the objective. The site of the ruined château had been formed into a redoubt with two concrete blockhouses. Charged with their destruction, 175 Tunnelling Company, Royal Engineers, with some difficulty, obtained supplies of the new explosive, ammonal. Unable to place separate charges under each blockhouse, they packed as much explosive as they could obtain into the tunnel 20 feet under one blockhouse and fired it as evening fell. Major S. H. Cowan of 175 Tunnelling Company witnessed the result from Brigade Headquarters about half a mile away.

given the horror that had just occurred, these events were, indeed, unremarkable. However, it must always be remembered that, when all was quiet on the Western Front, men were still suffering and dying in terrible circumstances.

The action on the Bellewaarde Ridge and at Hooge had left a curious appendix projecting into the lines of both British and Germans, for the latter had the ridge to the north and were on the west side of the lake but the British held the stables at Hooge Château (118b, p.36), while the Germans had the ruins of the château itself. If the Bellewaarde Ridge could be retaken and the line

…There was a cloud of smoke and dirt five hundred feet high, and an explosion and a real shake, *even* under our very feet. Then Hell was let loose and for twenty minutes every gun we had made a curtain of fire just beyond our objective.

The concrete emplacements were destroyed and the British seized the crater that replaced them, but could not advance further. On 30 July the Germans retaliated with a new weapon. The 8th Rifle Brigade had taken over the front line near the crater the previous evening and Second Lieutenant G. V. Carey's men were standing-to as dawn broke.

Left **The Ypres Salient in April 1917, largely as it had been 18 months before. German trenches in red, Allied in blue. For security reasons the Allies' trenches are not shown in full.**
Ordnance Survey map Belgium 28W, edition 5A. (TM)

Below **Men of the Honourable Artillery Company in front line trenches at Sanctuary Wood, July 1915. Compare with the modern photograph of the site, p.41.** (IWM Q.49382)

"There was a sudden hissing sound, and a bright crimson glare."

I started on the extreme right of my bit of the line to ensure that all my men were lining the trench with their swords [bayonets] fixed ... I decided to go on along ... a communication trench. There were servants and some odd men from my platoon in so-called "shelters" along there and I

Above **The surviving part of the Bremen Redoubt, behind the brickworks on the Frezenberg road on the outskirts of Zonnebeke.** (MFME Yp/Ar 2/30)

wanted to make sure these people who were apt to be forgotten at "stand-to" were all on the alert ... There was a sudden hissing sound, and a bright crimson glare over the crater turned the whole scene red. As I looked I saw three or four distinct jets of flame, like a line of powerful firehoses spraying fire instead of water, shoot across my fire trench.

The attack with "liquid fire" was immediately followed by shelling, grenades and a German infantry attack. The front line fell and the British had to withdraw to their support line. The counterattacks over the next few days did not succeed.

The first men of Kitchener's Army, the volunteers who had rushed to join the colours in 1914, were now reaching the front. Indeed, the attack on Hooge had been their first experience of combat in the Ypres Salient. Ernest Parker was 19

"We held our breath while stalwart fellows carried past blanketed forms."

pass us on their way back from the front line. Once or twice the words "Way for stretcher-bearers!" rang out, and we held our breath while stalwart fellows carried past blanketed forms aloft on their stretchers. How soon would it be our turn?

Above **British bunkers at Langhof Château, north of St Eloi. They now stand on private farmland and permission should be asked by anyone intending to visit them.** (MFME Yp/Ar 1/14)

Main Picture **The Somme: Men of the Wiltshire Regiment attack Thiepval, 7 August 1916.** (IWM Q.744)

years old when he arrived in the Salient with the 10th Durham Light Infantry.

At the close of that first day in Ypres we paraded for the nightly working-party in no man's land. With picks and shovels on our shoulders we passed through the Menin Gate and marched down the road as far as West Lane communication trench. Here we got under cover, filing along until we came to the front line. On our way we were continually halting, now to wait until the rear got into touch; now to allow troops to

Parker was amazed by the order to stand stock still when a flare went up, and by the adherence to this rule of the experienced men even when machine-guns were firing. They dug down to water-level when at last it was possible to risk a quick cigarette, crouched in the bottom of the trench. The experience of manning a front-line trench was one of constant tension, stealthy movement and the sickening smell of the unburied dead.

The Battle of Loos, north of Arras in France, began on 25 September. The British made their first use of poison gas, the chlorine killing 600 of

Stealthy movement and the sickening smell of the unburied dead.

the enemy and disabling 1,800. At first the advance was impressive, but the reserves were not released to General Haig soon enough and the action bogged down into a repetitive attack and counter-attack sequence that was to last until the end of the first week of October. German machine-guns were used with fearful efficiency. It was a weapon against which there was, for the time being, no answer.

On 15 December Sir John French resigned as and Commander-in-Chief on 19 December Haig was promoted to the position. General Joseph Joffre had been appointed Commander-in-Chief of all French armies on the Western Front on 3 November and sought Haig's agreement to undertake a massive campaign on the Somme in 1916. General von Falkenhayn and the German command were also making their plans. Frustrated by their failure to break the Allies, von Falkenhayn feared the British in the long term as the resources of the Empire were substantial and, in

addition, there was the threat of the United States entering the war. Russia was seen as a fading power racked by internal divisions, where revolution was a distinct possibility. He decided that he would concentrate German efforts against France, breaking the spirit of her people, and thus knock England's "best sword out of her hand". On 21 February the great attack began on an objective von Falkenhayn calculated the French would sacrifice everything to defend: Verdun. By the end of the battle, on 18 November 1916, the French losses would total 362,000 and the German 336,831.

In Britain the decision had been taken to regard France and Belgium as the priority. The

Above **The view from Hill 62, from which the Germans were able to overlook all movement south and west of Ypres. The towers of the Cloth Hall and the Cathedral rise above the wood in the distance, centre right. Perth (China Wall) Cemetery is on the left.** (MFME Yp/Ar 2/12)

Left **Company sergeant major, Grenadier Guards. The equipment is 1908-pattern, worn with a trench jerkin and rubber waders.**

(Osprey, Elite 61, *The Guards Divisions 1914-45*) (Mike Chappell)

Men succumbed to trench foot, influenza and paratyphoid.

abortive Gallipoli campaign had ended in January 1916 and the men of the Australian and New Zealand Army Corps, the ANZACs, were transferred to Haig's command. In the first six months of the year the BEF grew from three armies of 38 infantry divisions to four armies of 49 divisions. The number of cavalry divisions stayed at five.

In the Ypres Salient the harassment of the enemy was constant. Fortifications were improved, though more attention was given to this by the Germans than by the British. The former were determined to hold what they had gained and therefore built deep underground bunkers shored with timber and a web of concrete pillboxes and redoubts to secure their line. The British, on the other hand, were dedicated to the ejection of the invader from France and Belgium, and their trenches were seen as jumping-off points for an advance. Trench raids inflicted injury on the enemy and yielded prisoners for questioning. Mines and counter-mines were dug. Rain fell, trenches flooded, men succumbed to trench foot (similar to frostbite), influenza and paratyphoid. Lice infested their clothing. The conditions endured by soldiers of both sides were abominable. The Durhams and Ernest Parker were in the line near Boesinghe, (B11b, p.36).

Before our first march into the line, we changed into thigh boots, and by the time we reached it the ill-fitting boots (mine were size 10, but my feet were size 8) had nearly exhausted our strength ... My section crept out gingerly over the treacly mud and, one by one, jumped across a trench that was falling in. Missing my footing, I dropped into an oozing quagmire of mud, and my comrades, slithering in the mud on top, had to lie down and

"Missing my footing, I dropped into an oozing quagmire of mud."

attempt to tug me out. In doing so they pulled me clean out of my boots ... It was at Elverdinghe that we were first equipped with shrapnel helmets, yet another addition to the enormous load we carried wherever we went.

Operations were affected by the destruction of landmarks. Troops could be mistaken about their location and the messages sent to headquarters misleading, assuming they got through at all; telephone lines were cut by shellfire and runners killed in their attempts to carry messages. In

March 1915 the Germans had attacked at St Eloi on the Ypres–Wytschaete road at the junction with the Warneton road, creating a small salient. Five months later British tunnellers started sinking shafts some 50 feet deep and by the following March were under the German lines. At 4.15am on 27 March the bombardment started and six mines were blown. Mines 2 and 3 went up between the Wytschaete and Warneton roads, and 4 and 5 along the Hollebeke road, wiping out the two front-line companies of the 18th Reserve Jäger Battalion. West and east of them mines 1 and 6 blasted craters in no man's land. The British 9 Brigade occupied the first three craters and charged on to take the German third line. On their left two craters were seized, but they were not, as the occupants thought, 4 and 5, but 6 and an older hole later allocated the number 7. A gap divided the men of 9 Brigade, of which, for three days, they were unaware. The Germans got into

attacks and losses of the previous week had been based on wrong information. The Canadians suffered 1,373 casualties.

On 28 May 1916 General Alderson was replaced as commander of the Canadian Corps by Lieutenant-General the Hon. Sir Julian Byng. Soon after his appointment the Canadians faced their next big test. The 1st Canadian Division under Major-General Arthur Currie held the sector centred on Hill 60 and the 3rd Division under Major-General M. S. Mercer was to their left holding Mount Sorrel, Hill 61, Hill 62 and Sanctuary Wood. Behind Hill 62 the long finger of Observatory Ridge (124c, p.36) pointed to Ypres, making the hill and ridge a highly desirable prize for the Germans. The Canadians were aware of the preparations being made by XIII Württemberg Corps clearly directed at Hill 62. Royal Flying Corps observers had seen trenches strikingly similar to those occupied by the Canadians well behind the enemy line, a training

General Haig was in the process of building forces for the great battle on the Somme.

crater 5 and were not thrown out until 3 April. By that time the troops were exhausted and 6 Canadian Infantry Brigade took over the line, such as it was. Under constant artillery bombardment, directed by the Germans from the height of the Wytschaete-Messines Ridge, the Canadians laboured to construct a defensible line. By noon on 4 April half the men of the 27th Battalion (6 Brigade, 2nd Canadian Division) had been hit. During their relief the next night the Germans attacked and by the end of the night had regained all the ground previously lost to the British. The counter-attacks on craters 2 and 3 failed and, on the east, the same error of identification was made; 6 and 7 were mistaken for 4 and 5. It was not until Major J. A. Ross of the 24th Battalion made a personal reconnaissance on the night of 14-15 April that it was realised that the four central craters were all in German hands, and all the

ground for the attack. Early in the morning of 2 June Mercer and the commander of 8 Brigade, Brigadier-General V. A. S. Williams, set out to inspect their positions. They had just reached the trenches of the 4th Canadian Mounted Rifles in front of Armagh Wood when the German barrage began: shelling of unprecedented ferocity. Mercer was killed and Williams wounded, subsequently to be taken prisoner. The trenches and all in them were erased. For four hours the torrent of shells poured down on the Canadian line. Shortly after 1pm the Germans exploded four mines and four battalions, with another five in reserve, advanced, sweeping over Mount Sorrel and Hill 62, mopping up whatever resistance the handful of surviving defenders could offer. They swarmed on along Observatory Ridge and took a section of 4 Battery, Canadian Field Artillery, which the gunners defended with their revolvers to the last man.

To the rear of the 1st and 4th Mounted Rifles, the 5th checked the advance at Maple Copse. On the southern flank of the advance the 5th Battalion, Canadian Infantry machine-gunned the Württembergers and on the north Princess Patricia's Canadian Light Infantry poured a withering fire on the attackers. They were to hold this corner of Sanctuary Wood for the next eighteen hours, isolated and defiant, little groups defending blocked-off sections of the trenches. The PPCLI suffered over 400 casualties at Sanctuary Wood.

Brigadier-General E. S. Hoare Nairn of the Lahore Divisional Artillery was given temporary command of the 3rd Canadian Division that afternoon and was ordered by Byng to retake the ground that night. The additional forces allocated to him could not be assembled in time for the planned start and then the rockets to signal the attack failed to ignite; fourteen had to be used to

They were to hold ... for the next eighteen hours, isolated and defiant ...

make a six-rocket signal. The attack went in unco-ordinated and failed, although some 1,000 yards had been gained.

General Haig was in the process of building forces for the great battle on the Somme planned to take place later in the month and the reinforcements available were limited. However, the importance of the position was such that he gave General Plumer artillery in sufficient numbers for a greater concentration of firepower than the

Main picture **A tank prototype,**
Mother, **on trial in Hatfield
Park, Hertfordshire, between
29 January and 2 February
1916. The trailing wheels
were to assist steering and
were fitted to the Mark I
tanks that went into action on
the Somme in September;
later models did not have
them.** (TM001/B2)

On 15 September the British put a new weapon into action.

British had ever previously been able to bring to bear on the enemy. All that was needed was weather clear enough to permit registration of the guns on the new German positions. In the meanwhile they shelled known targets to the rear causing casualties in what the Germans described as horrifying numbers.

In the afternoon of 6 June the 28th Battalion (6 Brigade, 2nd Canadian Division), at Hooge, were shattered by the explosion of four great mines. The forward trenches were lost, but with the help of the 31st Battalion the support line was held. It was still vital to regain the high ground south of the Menin Road, and because of the losses his brigades had suffered General Currie regrouped them in two composite brigades. The attack was scheduled for 1.30am on 13 June.

Between 9 and 12 June four huge bombardments were inflicted on the Württembergers. Four times they steeled themselves to repel an attack that did not come. On 12 June the barrage lasted ten hours, and still no attack. That evening there was another half-hour of shelling and, after a further three-quarters of an hour of bombardment which ended just before zero hour, in heavy

rain, the Canadian attack went in. The Germans were unable to resist. Many of them were already dead and their trenches had been blasted out of existence. In an hour the Canadians had the hills.

Far to the south, on 1 July, the Battle of the Somme began. The French were not able to take a major role, beset as they were at Verdun. The British attack included a large proportion of Kitchener's Army battalions, new to war on this scale, and the preliminary bombardment had failed to clear the German wire from their path or

destroy the deep bunkers. The losses on the first day exceeded any the British Army had suffered in a single day before or were to endure since. In the long, costly advance that followed over the next four and a half months the British, Australians and Canadians sustained terrible casualties. There was, however, one ray of hope. On 15 September the British put a new weapon into action – the tank. The tanks were few and faulty, but the gains made against intense machine-gun fire on that day showed what might be done. How to misuse them would be demonstrated in the Ypres Salient.

THE BATTLE OF MESSINES RIDGE

Though by no means beaten, the rate of loss to the German Army on the Somme clearly could not be tolerated and, early in 1917, von Falkenhayn ordered a withdrawal to the prepared positions known to the British as the Hindenburg Line. These were, in fact, a series of complex entrenchments, barbed-wire barricades and strong points that formed a rough line from border to border across France. By this means the Germans maintained their presence on

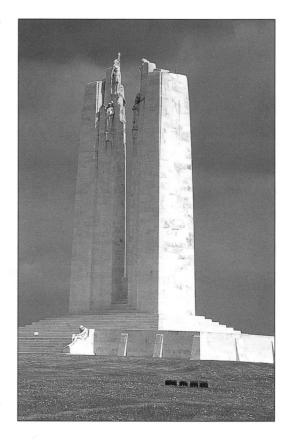

Early in 1917, von Falkenhayn ordered a withdrawal to the positions known to the British as the Hindenburg Line.

French soil with a significantly shortened line, reducing and simplifying lines of communication, and provided themselves with secure positions from which to repel attack and to mount their own offensives at the time and place of their choosing. Along the ridges and over the forward slopes of the Messines and Passchendaele Ridges the same attention to defensive works was given, creating a complex of wire, mutually supporting machine-gun posts and redoubts. The demands of the Eastern Front became a decreasing burden with the Russian Revolution of 12 March, although the formal ceasefire on that front was not to occur until December, after the October Bolshevik Revolution.

At the end of the previous year the French had managed to regain almost all the ground lost to the Germans at Verdun and the victorious gen-

eral, Robert Nivelle, now became Commander-in-Chief of the French Army in place of Joffre. He conceived a plan to launch a mighty attack on the German fortifications above the River Aisne, coordinated with an attack in Artois north of Arras on Vimy Ridge and also to the east of the town. The Canadians assaulted Vimy Ridge on 9 April and took it, gaining an eminence from which the southern hills below Ypres could be seen. To the east, on the River Scarpe, the attack by the British XVII Corps, part of Allenby's Third Army, was less satisfactory, bogging down in rain and snow, but none the less took 5,000 prisoners and moved the line forward significantly.

Chemin des Dames — Ferme de la Motte
The Farm of La Motte

Above **A relic of Nivelle's costly assault on the Chemin des Dames, April-May 1917; the ruins of the Ferme de la Motte.** (MFME Hist/Somme 2/7. HGG)

The French operation against the Chemin des Dames was a disaster.

The French operation against the Chemin des Dames was a disaster. On 20 April their Fifth and Sixth Armies made small gains but not the breakthrough Nivelle so confidently predicted. The Fourth and Tenth Armies were thrown into the conflict to no better advantage. The German losses were high at 163,000 but the French suffered even more, with 187,000 killed, wounded or taken prisoner. After two and a half years of war this proved to be the limit of the French troops' tolerance. At Châlons-sur-Marne on 29 April a unit declined to take orders, and the contagion soon spread. The "mutiny" was, in fact, largely limited to refusal to attack; defensive action continued so that the Germans were not aware of the problem. As the trouble grew, however, some men deserted. On 15 May Nivelle was relieved of his command and replaced by General Henri Philippe Pétain who had distinguised himself when he had commanded at Verdun. His task was not merely to bring the mutiny to an end, but to do so in a way that would restore the confidence and fighting spirit of the men. The situation reached a crisis on 27 May and Pétain acted firmly, having some 23,000 soldiers arrested and tried for mutiny and 400 of them sentenced to death. Only 50 were actually executed. At the same time he took positive action to improve the conditions of service. This, added to his reputation for doing all he could to preserve the lives of his troops, earned during

After two and a half years of war this proved to be the limit of the French troops' tolerance.

his command of the forces at Verdun, started the process of healing, but it would be a considerable time before the French Army was once again a robust force.

The burden of maintaining pressure on the German invaders of Belgium and France thus fell on the British. Hopes of bringing America into the war were increasing, but the speed with which that would have any practical effect would necessarily be modest. The German U-boats were destroying significant numbers of Allied ships bringing vital supplies to Europe, American vessels amongst them. The USA finally declared war on Germany on 6 April 1917, and the first American troops were in Paris on 4 July, but they could not make a contribution to the battle strength of the Allies until the following year.

The carnage of the Somme had shocked both the public and the politicians in Britain. The misleading, and often unjust, image of heedless generals demanding more and more men to thrust into the furnace of war to no good purpose was seductive, and thus it became increasingly difficult for the army to obtain the men and munitions required for the Western Front. Some influential politicians now saw involvement there as an unviable and disastrously costly stalemate; surely, the argument ran, operations elsewhere would prove more effective and less expensive. To many, including some senior commanders, the answer lay in knocking Turkey or Austria-Hungary out of the war, simply maintaining the BEF in France at a level sufficient to hold the Germans. However, Field Marshal Haig, as he had become in December 1916, was now free to act independently of the French and had at his command an army that was

Victory in Flanders would allow the British to wheel south and roll the German line up from north to south.

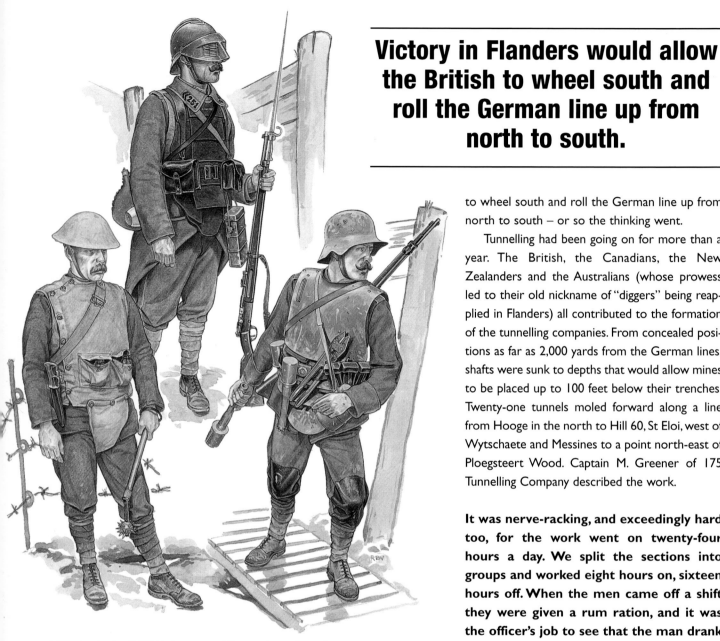

Above **Specialist troops equipped for raids.** Top: a French infantryman of the 251st Regiment in Lanciers body armour. Left: a British Mills bomber with a Chemico body shield. Right: a German storm trooper with body armour.

(Osprey, MAA 157, *Flak Jackets*)

(Ron Volstad)

to wheel south and roll the German line up from north to south – or so the thinking went.

Tunnelling had been going on for more than a year. The British, the Canadians, the New Zealanders and the Australians (whose prowess led to their old nickname of "diggers" being reapplied in Flanders) all contributed to the formation of the tunnelling companies. From concealed positions as far as 2,000 yards from the German lines, shafts were sunk to depths that would allow mines to be placed up to 100 feet below their trenches. Twenty-one tunnels moled forward along a line from Hooge in the north to Hill 60, St Eloi, west of Wytschaete and Messines to a point north-east of Ploegsteert Wood. Captain M. Greener of 175 Tunnelling Company described the work.

It was nerve-racking, and exceedingly hard too, for the work went on twenty-four hours a day. We split the sections into groups and worked eight hours on, sixteen hours off. When the men came off a shift they were given a rum ration, and it was the officer's job to see that the man drank his rum and didn't hoard it, because the pitmen had a habit of doing that.

An attempt to speed progress was made by the importation of an electrically driven boring

very different from that of a year earlier, hardened in the cauldron of the Somme and tested in the action in Artois. The artillery was improved in the number of guns available, their use and their ammunition. The infantry had learned new tactics and organisation. The tank existed.

Flanders was Haig's chosen area of operation. It was close to his supply lines, familiar to his staff, and offered the chance of a breakthrough that could put the Belgian coast in British hands, thus denying the Germans the use of the ports believed to be essential to the operation of U-boats. Victory in Flanders would allow the British

Right **The Messines Ridge at Wytschaete, marked for the attack of 7 June 1917. German trenches in red, British trenches in blue. Croonaert Chapel is at top centre and Spanbroekmolen, the Pool of Peace, and Lone Tree Cemetery are at N29d, just off this section of the map at the left. They can be visited by turning off the road west from Wytschaete, following the sign to the cemetery.** Ordnance Survey map Wytschaete 28 NO from 28SW2. (TM 107.3)

"It was nerve-racking, and exceedingly hard too, for the work went on twenty-four hours a day."

machine. It made very satisfactory progress when first it started work, but stuck fast when switched off to cool down. It was abandoned in the depths. The Germans were also digging, counter-mines aimed at the destruction of the British works and which might break into the tunnel or into which the British might themselves dig. The arrival of men who had worked on the digging of the London Underground, in similar soils, improved progress. Corporal T. Newell of 171 Tunnelling Company described the technique.

You lay on a wooden cross made out of a plank with the cross-strut just behind your shoulders. The cross was wedged into the tunnel so that you were lying at an angle of forty-five degrees with your feet towards the face. You worked with a sharp-pointed spade with a foot-rest on either side above the blade, and you drove the blade into the clay, kicked the clay out, and on to another section, moving forward all the time. With the old broad-bladed pick we could only get forward at best six feet on every shift, but when the clay-kicking method

was introduced we were advancing as much as twelve feet, or even fourteen, on a shift.

The spoil from these diggings had to be carried away from the workings and disposed of out of sight of the enemy and his reconnaissance aircraft. When the chambers dug out beneath the German lines were ready, the mines were charged with ammonal. The explosive was brought up by night in backpacks weighing 50 pounds and hauled through the tunnel to be packed into place and fused. One million pounds of ammonal was eventually placed in the workings, divided between 21 mines.

General Sir Herbert Plumer's Second Army was readied to make the attack; in the north XX Corps, in the centre IX Corps and in the south II ANZAC Corps. The preparations were meticulous. A model of Wytschaete was constructed behind the Café DeZonne in Dickebusch to allow the attackers to study the ground. The local citizens were well aware of it and the Germans were doubtless informed. On 15 May German counter-tunnelling near Hill 60 threatened the British mine there, but it was worked out that they would not progress fast enough to discover it before the attack. The possibility of a German withdrawal to safer positions was always present, however. For 17 days before the attack the artillery bombarded the German lines, and their guns replied.

At 3.10am on 7 June the charges were blown. The earth heaved as 19 huge mines went up; two failed. One of those blew up in 1955. Where the last one is no one knows. In Lille the German garrison, thinking they had been attacked, went to their stations. In England the shock was felt as an earthquake. Second Lieutenant J. W. Naylor of the Royal Field Artillery related his experience.

Our plunger [to detonate the mine] was in a dug-out, and the colonel and I were actually standing outside the dug-out because we both knew what was going to happen and we wanted to see as much as we could. The earth seemed to tear apart, and there was this enormous explosion right in front of us. It was an extraordinary sight. The

"With the old broad-bladed pick we could only get forward at best six feet on every shift."

Main picture **The spoil from tunnel workings had to be disposed of well away from the site to avoid detection. Troops supposedly resting from the front line spent weary hours carting it to the rear.** (IWM E(AUS).1681)

Inset **The Diggers. Australian tunnellers excavating dugouts at Hooge in September 1917. Broad-bladed picks are in use in the roomier conditions of the dugout.** (IWM E(AUS).E.2094)

Main picture **Mount Kemmel from Croonaert Wood, with Croonaert Chapel Cemetery among quiet fields.** (MFME Yp/Ar 1/11)

Below **Lone Tree Crater at Spanbroekmolen, now preserved as the Pool of Peace, and a pleasant place for ducks. The sap in which the mine was placed was started on 1 January 1916 and by 26 June 1916 it was 1,710 feet long and 88 feet deep. On June 1917 the mine, 91,000 pounds of ammonal, was detonated, blowing a hole 250 feet in diameter at ground level and 40 feet deep, and raising a rim 13 feet high and 90 feet wide. Everything within 430 feet of the explosion was entirely obliterated.** (MFME Yp/Ar 1/0)

whole ground went up and came down again. It was like a huge mushroom.

Taken together, these mines constituted the largest explosion, excepting nuclear devices, that has ever been contrived.

The British artillery's 2,266 guns went into action at once and the nine infantry divisions rushed forward, some so precipitately that they were injured by débris from the mines. The Germans in the front lines were entirely broken. It is estimated that 10,000 of them died or were buried alive in those first few seconds. The survivors were so dazed that they surrendered by the score – too numerous for men to be spared to escort them to captivity, so the New Zealanders cut off their trouser buttons and sent them back with both hands kept busy preserving their modesty. On Hill 60 the 12th Durham Light Infantry pushed forward as the 11th Prince of Wales's Own (West Yorkshire Regiment) secured the hilltop, digging new trenches facing east and, in Lieutenant J. Todd's words:

"The earth seemed to tear apart, and there was this enormous explosion right in front of us."

…We found a lot of German pillboxes up there and had to clear them out. There were quite a few Germans in them and we'd shout in to them to come out; if they didn't, then we chucked a bomb in. They came out fast enough then! It was eight or nine in the morning before we got properly dug in and by then the Germans had started a counter-barrage, so we were having some casualties.

By 7am the New Zealanders had taken Messines and the Australians were beyond Trench 127 near

Ploegsteert Wood. The British 25th Division took the ridge north of Messines. The 36th (Ulster) Division and the southerners, the 16th (Irish) Division, raced each other to Wytschaete and the ridge to its south. The 41st Division and, to their left, the 47th (1/2nd London) Division (Territorial Force) poured through between St Eloi and Hill 60 and further north again the 23rd advanced over the often-disputed ground south of the Menin Road. As the barrage moved forward and the infantry followed, the tanks moved up to support the follow-through to the trench lines beyond, supply tanks bringing up stores, while artillery batteries were also on the move to provide cover for the continuing advance. Corporal A. E. Lee of A Battalion, Heavy Branch, Machine-Gun Corps enjoyed the experience.

We each took our own route and we really felt we were coming into our own at last, being used properly at the right time on good ground.

Our job was simply to help the infantry. A runner came up and shouted, "We're held up by machine guns, over on the right." We went over, found that quite a lot of infantry were

"The whole ground went up and came down again. It was like a huge mushroom."

Above **Spanbroekmolen Cemetery lies above the shallow valley in front of Wytschaete and its church, on the horizon. The photograph was taken near the crossing of Narrow Reserve Trench and the road in N30d, see map p.49**

(MFME Yp/Ar 1/9)

"There was a farmhouse in the middle of it and behind that a wood, and all of a sudden machine-gun fire started spurting from this farmhouse."

Forward of Wytschaete and St Eloi, Corporal Lee in *Revenge* together with another tank, *Iron Rations*, patrolled while the troops dug in on the Green Line (see map, p.49). They had done their job, but decided to push on into German territory.

About five o'clock we came up to a field. There was a farmhouse in the middle of it and behind that a wood, and all of a sudden machine-gun fire started spurting from this farmhouse. We hadn't realised until then that it was a strongpoint, but we'd practised manoeuvres of this kind so often that we knew exactly what to do. We went left and *Iron Rations* went right and we started attacking the farmhouse from both sides. Well, after about half a dozen shells we must have hit something inflammable in the farmhouse ... Flames started belching out of one of the windows and to our absolute

Main picture **ANZAC officers watch the tanks advance to Messines Ridge, 7 June.** (TM 68/F3)

taking cover, and a hundred or so yards ahead we could see where the bullets were coming from. So we just drove straight at it, firing as we went, and of course that was the end of that.

By 3.15pm the whole ridge was secured and troops started moving down the eastern slope.

Right **A supply tank crosses the British line to follow up the attack on Messines Ridge. The sponsons have been closed off and the armament removed to make room for stores within. The camouflage netting is rolled on top.** (TM 53/G4)

Above **The New Zealand Memorial Park at Messines (Mesen) overlooks the steep little hill to the west which, from a car, appears so trivial. It is informative to try to run up it, even without a loaded pack on your back. German bunkers are now surrounded with flowering shrubs.** (MFME Yp/Ar 2/3)

Above right **The ruins of the Royal Institute and the Church at Messines.** (MFME Yp/Ar 1/34, courtesy M. Albert Ghekiere)

amazement we suddenly saw all these Jerries streaming out of the back door. There must have been two or three hundred of them, and they just bolted and ran and made for this wood about a hundred yards away. We both swung half-right, both tanks, and started firing at them in crossfire. Very few of them made it to the wood.

German counter-attacks on 8 June were thrown back by the well-entrenched victors of Messines Ridge and German Army Group Commander Crown Prince Rupprecht started planning for a withdrawal from the low land to the

east as far as the River Lys. By 11 June further advances had been made east of Messines so that the front line ran due south from Hill 60 as far as the River Douve before turning south-west to St Yvon and Ploegsteert Wood. The outstanding achievement brought joy to a British public hungry for good news, but there was still a substantial cost. British killed or wounded totalled 24,562, of whom 10,521 were ANZACs, and 11 tanks had been lost. The German head-count was slightly lower at 23,000, of whom 7,264 were made prisoner, and their material losses were 154 guns, 218 machine-guns and 60 mortars. It had not been a walk-over, but by the usual reckoning the BEF should have anticipated taking two to three times the casualties inflicted on the defenders, and most of the loss had been sustained in follow-up attacks to the taking of the ridge.

Plumer was restrained from developing his success. The purpose Haig had in mind was to straighten the Salient before making a major move on the hills further north and the Belgian coast. Instead of putting the operation in the hands of Plumer, who knew the Salient so well and had demonstrated his attributes of meticulous planning coupled with imaginative insight, he had decided to entrust the task to a man he considered more "thrusting", Lieutenant-General Sir Hubert Gough, a friend and fellow cavalryman.

Left **Men of the 33rd Battalion, Australian Infantry (9 Brigade, 3rd Australian Division), killed on 7 June 1917, lie shoulder to shoulder in Toronto Cemetery in the shade of Ploegsteert Wood.** (MFME Yp/Ar 1/25)

British killed or wounded totalled 24,562, of whom 10,521 were ANZACs, and 11 tanks had been lost.

Left **On the corner of Ploegsteert Wood the New Zealanders in Mud Corner Cemetery are overlooked by the Irish and British, and even a few Germans, at Prowse Point Cemetery.**
(MFME Yp/Ar 1/20)

THE THIRD BATTLE OF YPRES

The war on other fronts played its part in the course of the conflict in the Ypres Salient. On the Italian/Austrian front in the Trentino attack and counter-attack left 23,000 Italians and 9,000 Austrians killed or wounded for no significant change in the line. On the Eastern Front the Russians were under massive pressure and appeared to be crumbling. Although Pétain was rebuilding morale with personal visits to his divisions and improvements to the men's conditions, the French were still weakened by the disaf-

For six weeks after the triumph of Messines, in beautiful summer weather, men and matériel were massed for the onslaught.

fection of their troops. Haig answered the misgivings of his government with unflagging optimism for the success of his plans in the Salient, the best solution, in his view, to assisting the Allies on other fronts. For six weeks after the triumph of Messines, in beautiful summer weather, men and matériel were massed for the onslaught.

Right **Steenstraat, March 1917, from the album of M. Labyt. He captioned the picture: "Front line trench in the Redan, you will see the snow. Two men looking through a periscope to the German lines which are about 50 to 60 yards away. Just at the moment that I took this snap, the man on the left had a bullet through his helmet but was not wounded. Note the case of Mills hand grenades & on right a Projecteur." After the war Mr Labyt ran a private hotel in the rue St Pétersbourg, Ostend, advertised as having all modern conveniences, including indoor sanitation, and catering exclusively to British visitors, terms from 5 shillings per day inclusive.** (IFF)

Below **Steenstraat, Belgian front line trench. Two rifles with grenades, also Mills hand grenades. M. Labyt.** (IFF)

Overflying the area and observing from their lookouts on the Passchendaele Ridge, the Germans saw it coming.

Neither were the Germans idle. On 10 July they launched an attack at Nieuport, the extreme of the line on the Belgian coast, taking more than 1,000 prisoners. On 12 July they shelled the Salient, firing 50,000 rounds, and loosing a new horror – mustard gas. Nearly 2,500 soldiers were gassed, of whom 87 died. The mustard gas shells continued falling on British lines for the next three weeks, claiming another 14,726 victims, of whom 500 died. Staff Nurse C. Macfie described the scene at Godwaersvelt Casualty Clearing Station.

Above left **One of the largest surviving German bunkers stands north west of Pilckem. Leave the village by Bikschootestraat, go over the line of the old railway and turn immediately left on Slaakestraat. The bunker is on the left of the road.**
(MFME Yp/Ar 3/4)

Below left **British dugouts just north-west of Essex Farm Cemetery. The River Ieperlee and the Yser-Ypres Canal are beyond them to the right.**
(MFME Yp/Ar 3/1)

"The poor boys were helpless and the nurses had to take off these uniforms, all soaked with gas."

…The mustard gas cases started to come in. It was terrible to see them. I was in the post-operative tent so I didn't come in contact with them, but the nurses in the reception tent had a bad time. The poor boys were helpless and the nurses had to take off these uniforms, all soaked with gas, and do the best they could for the boys. Next day all the nurses had chest trouble and streaming eyes from the gassing. They were all yellow and dazed. Even their hair turned yellow and they were nearly as bad as the men, just from the fumes from their clothing.

On 17 July the British retaliated with a bombardment that was to last until the opening of the battle, firing 4,283,550 shells, including 100,000 containing chlorpicrin gas.

The attack planned by Field Marshal Haig was, however, still not a certainty. The agreement given in June by the British Government was conditional on the participation of the French, but this now seemed doubtful. On 20 July a half-hearted acquiescence was forthcoming from the British Government, provided that the attack would be called off if it did not go well. It was not until 25 July that full support for the plan was forthcoming.

The principal effort was to be made by Gough's Fifth Army between Zillebeke and Boesinghe, a front that included the rising ground of the ridge along the Menin Road to the Gheluvelt plateau in the south and the succession of undulations divided by a herringbone web of streams rising to Passchendaele in the north. To the left General

Below **Numerous pillboxes still stand on the Pilckem Ridge. This is one of a number along the Pilkem-Bikschoote road.**
(MFME/Yp/Ar3/7)

Below **British oblique photograph taken on 24 April 1917. Boesinghe (B11b, map p.36) is at the bottom left and the de l'Yser Canal runs across the centre, left to right, with German trenches on its far bank. The straight run to the horizon of the railway line to Roulers can be seen, with the Pilckem–Langemarck road weaving away to its right.** (TM 4511/D4)

"Very little could be seen, apart from the tangled coils of barbed wire."

François Anthoine's French First Army would secure the flank, while Plumer's Second Army was to perform the same function to the south. The BEF had 3,091 guns and 406 aircraft in the Ypres sector and Gough's Fifth Army nine divisions and 136 tanks. They faced the German Fourth Army with 13 divisions and some 600 aircraft and, in the south, six divisions of the Sixth Army.

Ernest Parker, was now commissioned, serving with the 2nd Royal Fusiliers. July was spent finding out what they could about the German positions.

Very little could be seen, apart from the tangled coils of barbed wire and the posts of the entanglements, but one object was prominent above the trench line. This was a flat-topped, concrete dug-out marking the nearest point of the German trenches at the very tip of the salient known as "Caesar's Nose" [C13b, page 36]... I made up my mind to visit this spot...

His first attempt at a night raid was frustrated by a British bombardment, but the next night he tried again.

Above and right **British oblique photograph of the approaches to Kitchener's Wood. The associated map demonstrates how oblique shots distort distances.** (TM 5410/A6 and 5410/B1)

I ... crept with two companions up to the German wire ... After watching for about half an hour, I decided to work forward and enter the trench ... I reached a hole into which I cautiously inserted my feet, crouching as low as possible while I worked my way forward. I was still struggling with the wire underfoot when a Very-light pistol cracked almost under my nose and its released flare soared above me high into the sky ... I distinguished first a dome-shaped helmet, then the face and features of a German soldier whose eyes were fixed, staring upwards at the curving path of the flare ... During this intolerable suspense my revolver pointed towards that unsuspecting face ... When after an eternity it was safe to move, I watched the head of the German sink down into the earth ...

It soon became evident that the soldier was moving from one position to another, shooting flare after flare, giving the impression of a heavily manned position. Parker led another raid, in greater force, a few nights later.

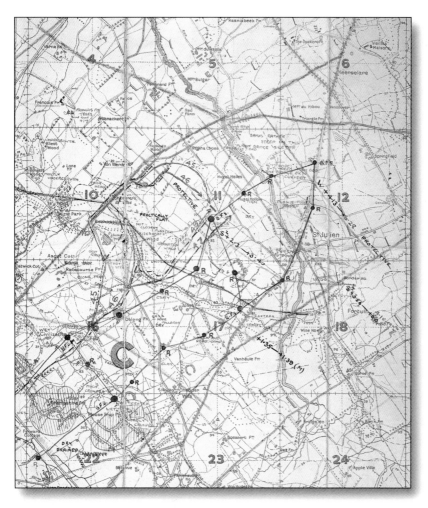

Above **Captain Kessel's map, marked with the routes planned for the tanks, G45, G46, G47 and G48, of 19 Company, Tank Corps, prior to the attack on 31 July (see p.66). German trenches in red, British in black (bottom left). Note the annotation and shading showing difficult ground.** Ordnance Survey map Pilckem, from 28NW2, trenches corrected to 11 July 1917. (TM 107.7)

Behind a creeping barrage, the shelling moving forward at a steady pace...

Anticipating attack on 28 July, the Germans withdrew from some 3,000 yards of their trenches opposite Boesinghe the night before. The French and the Guards Division took advantage of this error and crossed the canal immediately, took over the trenches and began building bridges to reinforce this unexpected improvement in their start line.

They found the trenches they entered empty, blocked in places by earth heaps thrown up by British shells, and in the form of breastworks revetted with brushwood fascines. He assumed occasional working-parties were sent out to keep them in repair. They found a number of empty dugouts before coming on a solitary German soldier whom they took prisoner. The rest of the German patrol came up and were sent running with a fusillade of shots and a shower of bombs. One aspect of the German scheme of defence was clear: the front line at least consisted of strong pillboxes for machine-guns and almost empty trenches to be manned only when necessary. Parker comments that, as the day for the attack approached, the weather broke and the rain continued until 31 July. Indeed, on the day of the attack itself over three-quarters of an inch (21.7mm) of rain soaked the battlefield.

At 3.50am on 31 July the Third Battle of Ypres began. Behind a creeping barrage, the shelling moving forward at a steady pace with which the troops could keep up, the advance was swift. In the north the Guards Division moved forward from Boesinghe to the left of the railway line, meeting little resistance and attaining their first objective, the Black Line, by 5am. They stayed in touch with the French to their left, and although they were checked by machine-gun fire from blockhouses from time to time, by about 8.30am they were on the ridge overlooking the Steenbeek. An hour later 1st Guards Brigade, in support, had a company digging in beyond the stream. On their right the 38th (Welsh) Division had a harder time. They met the first solid resistance in attempting to take Iron Cross, which

eventually fell to the 14th Welsh Regiment, and the ridge. The 11th South Wales Borderers and the 17th Royal Welsh Fusiliers had to deal with the pillboxes in the fortified farms along the ridge before they could achieve their objective, the crossing of the Steenbeek.

The 51st (Highland) Division also ran into pillbox trouble as they gained the ridge on the right of the 38th. The 1/6th Seaforth Highlanders and the 1/6th Gordon Highlanders took Macdonald's Wood and Farm (C10a, opposite) with help from tank G50. Alongside them to the south-east the 39th Division were advancing over the ground towards Kitchener's Wood which the Canadians had taken so gallantly two years earlier; four tanks of G Battalion, Tank Corps, were in support. The Tank Corps was only four days old; previously it

Below **The site of Kitchener's Wood. The area marked "sunken, wet" (C10d) on Kessel's map is now a pond. The windmill on the site of the Totemühle, the "Deathmill" used earlier as an artillery observation post, east of Vancouver, is to the right of the tree.** (MFME Yp/Ar 3/9)

had been known as the Heavy Branch, Machine-Gun Corps, a name adopted for purposes of secrecy at their formation.

Captain D. G. Browne, MC, wrote of his service in the war and left a detailed account of the operation from the tank man's point of view. His section of 19 Company received the following orders:

After crossing the front line, No. 10 Section will split up. The left-hand pair, G45 and G46 [Browne's tank], pass to the north of Kultur Farm and take the northern end of Kitchener's Wood, giving special attention to Boche Castle and strong-point; then proceed round the wood and mop up in conjunction with the infantry until the barrage at line S lifts at zero plus 4.1, when they will advance with the infantry, giving special attention to Regina Cross. The right-hand pair, G47 and G48, passing to

"A grisly conglomeration of mounds of mud and pools of water."

the south of Kultur Farm, will take the southern end of Kitchener's Wood, and on the lifting of the barrage on line S at zero plus 4.1, will devote their attention to the strong-point at Alberta, and push forward at the discretion of the commander towards Hugel Hollow. As soon as the infantry are consolidated on the Steenbeek

Line, tanks will rally at C11d 20.90 (north of Alberta).

As examination of Browne's commanding officer's – Captain Kessel's – marked-up map for the operation shows, this was not as simple as it sounds. Browne points out that the approach was between Canadian Farm (C15d), which is annotated "flooded except in dry weather", and Hampshire Farm (C22a), "wet". Neither existed as a farm any more, merely as ruins. Moreover, by the time the bombardment had passed, any firm ground would have been reduced to "a grisly conglomeration of mounds of mud and pools of water". The landmarks that might be of some use in navigating a machine with restricted vision would almost certainly have been destroyed. Intelligence Branch provided them with helpful little sketches, including one of Hooglede Church. That turned out to be in a village north-west of Roulers, some nine miles beyond the objective.

As a sign of optimism in high quarters this valedictory gift was appreciated; but, being under no delusions ourselves as to the difficulties before us, we felt that there was small hope of visiting the place in the immediate future.

Browne started his approach on the evening of 28 July, in the dark, making his way with the rest of the company over tracks pitted with holes and flanked by entrapping mud, finding a way through the heavy traffic of men and supplies also on the move under cover of darkness. A light railway engine on one of the railroads built to move supplies collided with one tank, another two slid off the timbered road and had to be unditched. In all it took seven hours to move 5,000 yards. They laid up under camouflage netting during the next day and moved on once more at 11pm to a position some 300 yards from Forward Cottage (C21b) where they would cross the line.

Below **G46, D. G. Browne's tank, bogged down before it had got to Adam's Farm (C10b), on the left of the road. It was photographed some ten weeks later, having suffered shell damage to a track in the meantime.** (TM 867/A4)

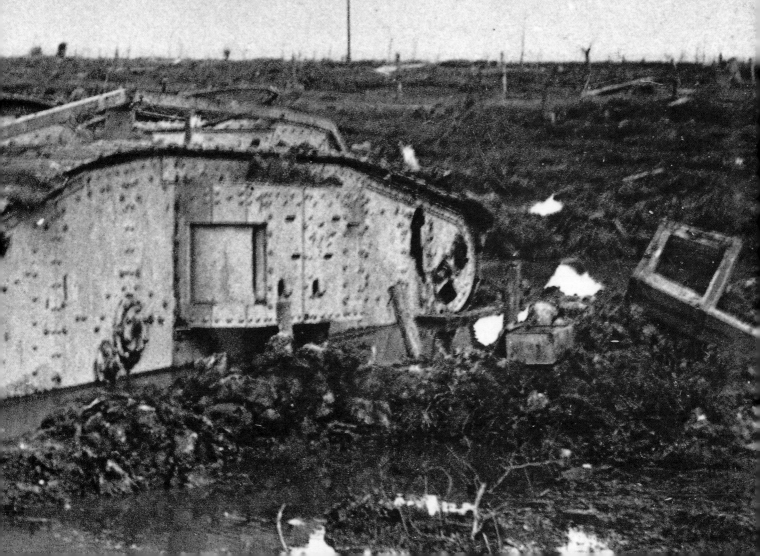

The passage between Hampshire and Canadian Farms exceeded even Browne's worst expectations.

The front line was not merely obliterated: it had been scorched and pulverised as if by an earthquake, stamped flat and heaved up again, caught as it fell and blown all ways; and when four minutes' blast of destruction moved on, was left dissolved into its elements, heaped in fantastic mounds of mud, or excavated into crumbling pits already half full of water ... Before us yawned a deep muddy gulf, out of whose slimy sides obtruded fragments of splintered timber, broken slabs of concrete, and several human legs clothed in German half-boots.

They were guided across the remains of the barbed wire which had survived in one place sufficiently to give them grip, and pushed on up the slope into the dawn. Just over an hour after starting they recognised the outline of Kitchener's Wood and heard, for the first time, the rattle of shell fragments on the hull of the tank. At this point the unditching beam (see illustration below), its lashings cut by those same splinters, toppled off in front of them. They wasted no time in trying to recover it. At 5.15am they came up to Boche Castle (C10d) and, having been warned that the light railway on the road known as Boundary Road, along the north end of the wood, was mined, made for the ground to its left. It was peppered with shell-holes turning into ponds with slides of mud in between.
Attempts to gain

Below **An exercise in the use of a tank's unditching beam, photographed in February 1918. The tracks drew the beam under the tank and the super-structure is fitted with rails on to which it is eventually pulled as the tank moves forward, to be unshackled and tied down before the machine proceeded.** (TM866/D2)

Water flowed in, flooded the clutch and engine, and the tank stuck.

the roadway and risk mines were futile; the tank could not get enough grip to change direction. Eventually, alongside the wood, a shell-hole proved too deep, the water flowed in, flooded the clutch and engine, and the tank stuck. Browne and one of his men stayed with G46, the others going to the rear, and the next day a recovery officer, the rain pouring off his waterproof, solemnly suggested they bail out the shell-hole with fuel cans. Only one tank in Browne's section had any success, John Alden's. He reached Alberta, assisted the infantry in taking it, and then took part in a gunnery duel with an armoured light train on the other side of the Steenbeek, putting it to flight. As an illustration of the incompatibility of rain, intense artillery bombardment and the effective use of tanks, the operation was perfect.

In contrast to the satisfactory progress on the first day of the battle in the northern sector, events unfolded less favourably along the Menin Road.

Enemy shellfire delayed the advance of the 30th Division through Sanctuary Wood and in the subsequent rush forward the regiments got mixed up. Half of the 18th King's (Liverpool Regiment) made it from their start line on Observatory Ridge to a position just south of Stirling Castle (J13d, p.73), but the other half veered left and ended up at Clapham Junction. A mixed group of the 2nd Wiltshire Regiment, the 19th Manchester Regiment and the 2nd Royal Scots Fusiliers were held up by machine-gun fire from Sterling Castle but, with the support of 89 Brigade who were in reserve, eventually took it. By then the damage done by the German machine-gunners was severe. The 2nd Royal Scots Fusiliers entered Château Wood (J13a) north of the Menin Road in the belief it was Glencorse Wood (J14b) and reported their success accordingly. It was to prove an expensive error.

North of the road the 2nd Northamptonshire Regiment took Bellewaarde Lake and, with the 1st Worcestershire Regiment, Bellewaarde Ridge where the 1st Nottinghamshire and Derbyshire Regiment (Sherwood Foresters), passing through them, came under heavy fire from the direction of

"There was machine-gun fire, not just from their positions ahead of us but coming from outposts all round about."

the Hanebeek and from Glencorse Wood. Private W. Lockey gave this account.

...As we got further into their lines there was more and more machine-gun fire, not just from their positions ahead of us but coming from outposts all round about ... The fellows coming up behind us had a really rough time. We got into our position on the Westhoek Ridge, took over some trenches and dug-outs, and another division was supposed to pass through us and carry on the advance. While we were waiting it began to rain ... When they [the 1st Royal Irish Rifles] reached us they were in a bad way. The majority were either knocked out or wounded by the German machine-guns. Three or four staggered into our trench and every one had bullet-wounds in the arms or legs ... We couldn't get the wounded away, not from that point, for there was nothing between us and the Germans. They were pasting us with shells and machine-gun fire and the rain kept pouring down. The trench began to fill up with water.

The same fate befell 23 Brigade to their left. Neither it nor 24 Brigade could make further progress and they were forced to take cover behind Westhoek Ridge.

Corporal A. E. Lee of 3 Company, Tank Corps was making for Surbiton Villas (J13b), north-west of Clapham Junction, in *Revenge*. When they left the Menin Road and turned towards Surbiton Villas and Glencorse Wood they became ditched. The Germans gathered to counter-attack and Lee could see them clambering out of their trenches. Lee and Pat Brady got out of the tank, taking two machine-guns, and moved away from the stranded machine.

They started coming towards us. We waited – it seemed like hours – until the Germans were at point-blank range. Then we let them have it. They were probably expecting fire from the tank and instead were

caught in crossfire from hidden positions in front ... The infantry arrived and took the survivors prisoner ...

At that moment *Iron Rations* came up, and Lee went about borrowing its unditching beam to add to his own in order to get *Revenge* out. As he was doing so the second tank took a direct hit from a shell. Lee was thrown aside, but the tank was a complete wreck and all the crew killed. Lee managed to get his tank on the move once more and withdrew to base.

Plumer's Second Army also attacked on 31 July, making an advance on the whole length of their front from the New Zealanders towards Warneton in the south to the 41st Division astride the Ypres-Comines Canal.

Gough could consider the day's achievements with a certain satisfaction. The ground gained in the north was substantial. However, where it mattered most, along the Menin Road and towards the Gheluvelt plateau, things had gone awry. And still it rained.

The first week of August was marked by continuous, unseasonal rainfall, though it was as forecast by the meteorologists. By the middle of the month the Salient was to be subjected to more than three and a half inches, over 90mm, of rainfall, filling the shell-holes with water and turning the earth to a glutinous soup. The Germans counter-attacked repeatedly, at times gaining a little ground only to be driven back once more, at other times failing as the combination of accurate artillery and machine-gun fire cut them down. The advance, however, had ceased. The first phases of Third Ypres had cost the British 31,850 killed and wounded.

On 7 August the 2nd Royal Fusiliers relieved the Guards and Ernest Parker, now wearing the ribbon of the MC, was told by a Guards officer that a counter-attack across the Steenbeek was expected. In the dark Parker went forward to investigate.

... I took six men and approached this bridge until I distinctly heard this blood-

chilling sound of loud whispering coming from the other side of the stream ... With great caution I crossed the stream and climbed the slope on the far side. On the crest of the ridge was a line of trees linked by small bushes and some wire, and when I stood against the nearest of the trees, peering round the trunk with a loaded revolver in readiness, two figures rose from the ground so that I fired my revolver instinctively. All round figures got up hastily from behind the bushes, and as they made off with the sound of a flight of birds, the men behind me opened up a heavy fire with their rifles. When I stopped to reload my revolver two rifles were rested on my shoulders, the men using my body as a support to steady their aim ... What surprised me so much was the size of the party that fled so precipitately; there must have been more than forty of them.

What Parker had discovered was the essential of the German defensive tactic: counter-attack in strength combined with fortified strongpoints.

The lack of progress along the Menin Road was to be corrected on 10 August. The 7th Queen's (Royal West Surrey) Regiment moved into their start positions by moonlight, but were seen and cruelly savaged by shellfire. They were supposed to form the southern flank at Inverness Copse straddling the Menin Road, but even their efforts to work round the eastern side were stopped by machine-gun fire. On their left, but out of touch, the 11th Royal Fusiliers got further forward in the gap between Inverness Copse and Glencorse Wood but were driven back beyond Clapham Junction. The 7th Bedfordshire Regiment actually held Glencorse Wood for a while, but their exposed flank, where the Fusiliers should have been, laid them open to attacks that pushed them out of the wood. To the left again, between the Bedfords and the railway, the 25th Division attacked with greater success. The 2nd Royal Irish Rifles swept in to Westhoek and, protected as they were by the flooded valley of the Hanebeek

from German counter-attacks, consolidated the position. It was a small gain.

It just went on raining and that same quagmire that had served to defend Westhoek had to be crossed in the attack of 16 August, an operation that came to be known as the Battle of Langemarck. Inverness Copse and Glencorse Wood were entered once again, and once again lost. Formations advancing were pushed off line by the absolute necessity to go round lakes of mud up to four feet deep. It was reported that some valiant souls had actually entered the north of Polygon Wood, but, as they were never seen again, one cannot be sure. The best progress south of the railway was a mere 400 yards. North of the railway the attack at 4.45am moved forward briskly, but was soon under heavy fire from blockhouses. They dug in and many held on all day, but the failure of flanking units meant that they were all back at the start line by the end of the day. South of St Julien 109 Brigade's 14th Royal Irish Rifles and 11th Royal Inniskilling Fusiliers secured Fort Hill and Corn Hill. They too dug in.

Lieutenant Edwin Vaughan of the 1/8th Royal Warwickshire Regiment had discussed the terrain with his fellow officers a couple of weeks earlier.

Ewing was sorting out maps for us, and as we gathered round a large-scale trench map of Pilckem [see map, p.64], he said he had no definite news for us. He only knew that in about a week or ten days, we would be taking part in an attack somewhere along the Steenbeck [sic] stream. But he confirmed Pepper's statement that the German defences consisted of enormous concrete blockhouses so situated that the guns mutually enfiladed each other. I felt a terrible sinking inside when I heard this, for it appeared that any attack must be unsuccessful, but when we had discussed it exhaustively we came to the conclusion that the reports must be exaggerated, and we decided not to worry about them.

> "I distinctly heard this blood-chilling sound of loud whispering coming from the other side of the stream."

Below **The Royal Engineers at work on 3 August 1917 on a bridge over the Canal de l'Yser Canal to augment the flow of men and supplies to the front.** (IWM Q.5859)

"...the whole earth burst into flame with one tremendous roar as hundreds of guns hurled the first round of the barrage."

It took a little longer than a week or ten days before Vaughan had the opportunity to put their conclusions to the test. At 2am on 16 August the 1/8th Warwicks moved out of camp and over Bridge 2A on the Yser Canal. The stench was intolerable; the water was filled with broken wagons and guns and with the bodies of men and horses. They moved on and in the shelter of the bank by the canal towpath took comfort from a hot breakfast of sausages and bacon provided from the mobile cookers. At 4.45am "...the whole earth burst into flame with one tremendous roar as hundreds of guns hurled the first round of the barrage." The Company moved forward through the batteries to a sleeper track, a wooden road, up which they marched in fours, singing. The track deteriorated into shell-holes and mud as they approached Van Heule Farm (C17d, p.64), the first pillboxes, where they deployed in artillery formation to the right of the road and continued forward towards the shellfire, taking cover in shell-holes just thirty yards short of the "...terrible curtain through which we must soon pass".

To their south were 109 Brigade (36th [Ulster] Division) and in the north the line stretched beyond Langemarck. Vaughan was close to the centre, to the right of the ruins of St Julien (C12c). As machine-gun fire started to pass above them he was ordered to send a patrol to locate Border House (C18b) and then to move up to occupy the position. Corporal Wood found it and they stepped out into the enemy barrage to climb the shallow ridge before them. Mud became a friend; shell-bursts were muffled by the ooze but many men fell. Vaughan himself sank into the morass to his waist before he was pulled clear and ran to follow his men through a gap in the barbed wire. Just as they reached the shelter of Steenbeek (C18b), the stream that ran across their line of advance, a shell blew Corporal Breeze into the air, terribly wounded. From the cover of the sunken watercourse, which they found occupied by men of the 14th Irish Rifles, they saw a movement of Breeze's torn body and the stretcher-bearers rushed to him.

Very gently they brought him in to where I was sitting. He was terribly mutilated, both his feet had gone and one arm, his legs and trunk were torn to ribbons and his face

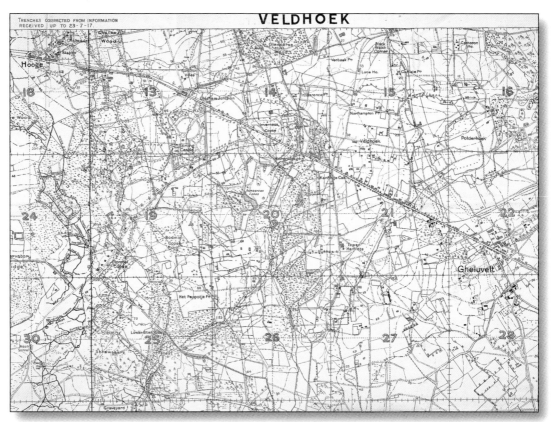

was dreadful. **But he was conscious and as I bent over him I saw in his remaining eye a gleam of mingled recognition and terror. His feeble hand clutched my equipment, and then the light faded from his eye. The shells continued to pour but we gave poor Breezy a burial in a shell-hole and the padre read a hurried prayer.**

The major in command of the Irish Rifles told Vaughan that he was moving no further and in fact the advance south of their position had stalled entirely. He had Vaughan move a little to the left and the Warwicks manned the bank along the edge of the stream while a runner attempted to re-establish contact with the rest of the company. They soon found 14 Platoon and made a ragged line from shell-hole to shell-hole. No one had even seen the enemy so far. It was now early afternoon, and as the bombardment eased they had a meal. At about 3.30pm Vaughan was ordered to take over command of the company and to move to the left that evening, form up behind the 1/5th

Gloucestershire Regiment and go forward after dark to tackle machine-gun positions. Mud and machine-gun fire made the task impossible. The Gloucesters had done well, establishing a line from Border House to St Julien, and in the shelter of this Vaughan and his men settled down as dawn broke, to hold it when the Gloucesters moved out.

The further north the line stretched, the better things went. The blockhouses along the St Julien to

Poelcapelle road, Maison du Hibou and the Triangle, held the right of 34 Brigade back, but on the left they went as far forward as Pheasant Trench, although Rat House remained in enemy hands. Langemarck itself fell by about 7am and the advance continued well beyond, though subject to strong counter-attacks. Only on this flank of the day's attack was any solid success achieved – Langemarck was in British hands. On the southern flank, the most important, there was failure. Calling it the Battle of Langemarck could not change that.

The 17th was quiet all morning and on into the afternoon. Vaughan, exhausted, dazed and sleepless, looked out from his hole.

There was just a dreary waste of mud and water, no relic of civilisation, only shell-holes and faint mounds behind the German lines. And everywhere were bodies, English and German, in all attitudes and stages of decomposition. No sign anywhere of a living man or gun.

A brief bout of shellfire in the middle of the afternoon over to the north was followed by more silence until dark when, after making contact with the 1/4th Oxfordshire and Buckinghamshire Light Infantry on his left, Vaughan treated himself to a supper of bread and cheese with a draught of cold tea out of a petrol can. A cigarette and a tot of whisky completed the meal.

Left **Salvation Corner (I1d, map p.36), 3 August 1917. A 12-inch Mark I howitzer, on a railway mounting, of 104 Siege Battery, Royal Garrison Artillery.** (IWM Q.6458)

Above **The Steenbeek and St Julien today from the south west, with the windmill beyond, taken from the point at which the road and the stream come together (C17d). It was in this gully that Edwin Vaughan and his men of the 1/8th Royal Warwickshires took cover on 17 August.** (MFME Yp/Ar 3/16)

At 2am on 18 August the Warwicks spread out to form a line with the Oxford and Bucks and waited for the light. When it came they waited on, gazing at a landscape full of corpses and the gruesome wreck of a burnt-out tank complete with blackened crew. At 3.30pm the British artillery fired ranging shots on the Winnipeg Crossroads (C12d), provoking retaliatory fire from the Germans. The day drifted away with no movement in this sector, although to the south, along the Menin Road, 43 Brigade made some modest progress at Inverness Copse with the help of two tanks. By 7pm it was dark enough to leave the cover of the shell-holes and walk about, and as night fell the 1/6th Warwicks came up to relieve them.

The blockhouses on the St Julien-Poelcapelle road still precluded forward movement. The cost of an infantry attack was obviously going to be severe, if not intolerable. It was decided to try the much-maligned tanks against Maison du Hibou (C6c) and The Cockcroft (C6a). The tanks of 19, 20 and 21 Companies were to move along the roads, or what remained of them, accompanied by a platoon of the 1/8th Worcestershire Regiment and the 7th Royal Warwickshire Regiment to each tank, keeping 250 yards behind, and briefed to come up to occupy the objective or help the tank when a shovel was waved out of the manhole on the tank roof. There was to be no artillery preparation: this was a surprise attack. A creeping barrage was to accompany the advance with smoke laid on the enemy third-line trenches to conceal what was taking place. The tanks had started to move into position at 8.30pm on 17 August. The shattered roads were crammed with men and mules, slipping and struggling to carry supplies up and the wounded down the line. It took them five and half hours to move forward 2,500 yards. The following morning they left their tanks at Bellevue (C22d) and went back to base for a wash and a rest.

At 8pm on 18 August the crews set off to their tanks. Two machines were allocated to each major target, the Cockcroft, Maison du Hibou, Triangle Farm and Vancouver (C6c), and one each for Hillock Farm and for the gunpits on the opposite

There was to be no artillery preparation: this was a surprise attack.

side of the Poelcapelle road (C12a). Browne, in G47, was allocated the gunpits. Only two male tanks, the designation of machines with 6-pounder guns, were available so the force relied mainly on females, armed with machine-guns. They moved off shortly after 1am on 19 August up to St Julien and crossed the Steenbeek with difficulty about 100 yards to the left of the old bridge in St Julien where the engineers had laid fascines. The temporary bridge sank under their weight and two tanks, including a male earmarked for the attack on the Cockcroft, ditched. As dawn broke they were pushing up the road, keeping to the pavé in the centre which had survived better than the tarmac at the sides; beyond that it was mud and standing water, undrainable because of the shelled, blocked ditches. Browne became aware of the rattle of bullets on his tank (G47) and his Lewis-gunners opened fire. He could not get close to his target because of the bog that separated it from the road, so a long-distance exchange continued for a while and then the rattle ceased. Near the gunpits "a great plume of smoke and mud shot suddenly upward … a second plume, and a third." The Germans were shelling the position, presumably now abandoned. G44 had dealt with Hillock Farm and the two machines turned to the rear, the infantry occupying the objectives. At the Cockcroft the female tank had become ditched, but not before it had succeeded in getting within 50 yards of the target. The garrison fled. The male tank attacking the Maison du Hibou had also bogged down, but was still able to open fire with its 6-pounder. Under this attack the Germans emerged to be killed or captured. Triangle Farm and Vancouver were also taken. The total British

… gun limbers and supply wagons choked the road.

casualties for the operation came to a mere 15 wounded. The time was 7am. It was a convincing vindication of the use of tanks.

The grim battle was still far from over. On 21 August the effort was renewed from the Menin Road in the south to the Triangle in the north. The 13th Royal Scots and the 11th Argyll and Sutherland Highlanders launched themselves at Potsdam (D26c, p.84), Vampir (D26a) and Borry Farm (D25b), and apparently took them, but were cut down by machine-gun fire and the few survivors fell back. Near St Julien some progress was made against Winnipeg but Springfield (C12b, p.64) stood firm against the Warwicks. Further south the remorseless battle for Inverness Copse and Glencorse Wood persisted with more heavy losses of men and no gain of ground.

On 25 August at 8pm Vaughan led his company forward once more, by the same route as he had followed nine days before, to virtually the same place, St Julien, and installed them in a bunker known as the Boilerhouse. It had been a quiet day with few attacks on the German line. The 9th Black Watch had made an attempt to take Gallipoli (D13d). They gained 170 yards. In the night the rain started again; three-quarters of an

inch would fall that Sunday. The shelling was continuous. The holes filled with water. Vaughan played cards and slept through the day.

The plan was for the 7th Warwicks to take the German line from Winnipeg (D7c, p.84) to Triangle Farm (C6c, p.64), then the 1/8th were to seize the Langemarck Ridge from Arbre (D7a, p.84) to Genoa Farm (D1c, p.96) and the 4th Royal Berkshire Regiment would take the final objective of Von Tirpitz (D7b) and Hubner (D1c) Farms. The 1/8th Warwicks formed up at 10.30pm and their machine-guns were brought into action to cover the noise of the approaching tank support.

Rations, cookers, gun limbers and supply wagons choked the road. Vaughan received his orders. He was to move at 1.45pm the next day – a daylight attack. A fellow officer wrote out an indent for 96 pairs Waterwings, Mark III, but decided HQ might not appreciate it. Monday 27 August dawned raining; a further half-inch was to be the day's ration, with sunshine in the intervals.

The British barrage accompanied the advance – as did the German. Vaughan was sure they must have known of the plan. In five minutes his line had dissolved. Four tanks ground past but two were halted almost immediately. The men took what

Main picture **British troops occupy one of the innumerable German gun emplacements that hampered their advance.** (TM410/E6)

Below and opposite **Heavy
artillery pulverised the
ground, as comparison of
these two British aerial
photographs shows. The area
can be seen on the Veldhoek
map, p.73, squares 15 and 21.
Northampton Farm (J15c) is
at the top of the picture
below, dated 7 July 1917. The
German trenches run up the
road to the right. The second
photograph, opposite, dated
10 August, is of the central
portion of the first, now
entirely covered with shell
holes.**

(TM 5410/A3 and 5410/A2)

The shelling was continuous. The holes filled with water.

cover they could while their barrage crept away towards the ridge. By 6.30pm the situation appeared unchanged and Vaughan ran and floundered his way to the gunpits where he was told to take his men to the Triangle and attack the pillbox at Springfield (C12b). He found only 15, either fit or willing to go with him and took them over to the remaining tanks, but the machines were attracting German fire and he pushed his men on.

Up the road we staggered, shells bursting around us. A man stopped dead in front of me, and exasperated I cursed him and butted him with my knee. Very gently he said "I'm blind, Sir," and turned to show me his eyes and nose torn away by a piece of shell. "Oh God! I'm sorry, sonny," I said. "Keep going on the hard part," and left him staggering back in his darkness.

The enemy fire was lighter at the Triangle and men who had been pinned down, 8th Worcesters and 7th Warwicks, rose to join Vaughan's group. A tank was moving around behind Springfield and opened fire, only to be shattered by a German shell. The tank had, however, accomplished its mission, having fired clean through the pillbox door. The enemy fire died away and the pillbox spewed out its defenders, hands above their heads, to be ordered to the British rear. As they set out, in the growing darkness, a German machine-gun cut them down. Inside the pillbox Vaughan found a wounded German officer, mortified at his failure to hold the position. He made him as comfortable as he could before flashing signals to the rear to

"It was too horribly obvious that dozens of men with serious wounds must have crawled for safety into new shell-holes, and now the water was rising about them."

identify their position. There was no acknowledgement. He stepped outside now that the gunfire had died away.

From the darkness on all sides came the groans and wails of wounded men; faint, long, sobbing moans of agony, and despairing shrieks. It was too horribly obvious that dozens of men with serious wounds must have crawled for safety into new shell-holes, and now the water was rising about them and, powerless to move, they were slowly drowning ... And we could do nothing to help them ...

At last, at 11.15pm, relief arrived and the Warwicks made their way to the rear. The torn land was scattered with wounded who begged help they could not give. Out of the 90 men with whom he had started only a day or two ago, Vaughan had 15 effectives left.

On the Menin Road the line stood much as it had before the battle began. It was said that Glencorse Wood had changed hands 19 times. In the north Langemarck itself had fallen and an advance of some 4,000 yards had been achieved. In the centre Springfield, an early objective, had fallen at last. But this was the work of nearly four weeks' fighting, fighting which had cost the British 68,010 killed, wounded or missing, and the gains were not impressive.

Field Marshal Haig was by now disenchanted with Gough. The latter's reputation as a thruster had not been justified by events, though who could thrust in the prevailing conditions is rather difficult to understand. The impasse on the Menin Road was more than serious – it threatened the whole campaign with failure. No doubt Gough found himself relieved in more ways than one when he was asked to agree to Plumer extending the Second Army front northwards to take on the problem.

PASSCHENDAELE

Main picture **Supply dumps along the Menin Road, photographed in September 1917.** (TM 5410/B5)

Right **The 1st Australian Division moving up from Hooge to Stirling Castle on 20 September 1917.** (TM 4511/D2)

At Verdun the French had, by 28 August 1917, regained almost all the ground they had lost since the first German onslaught on 21 February 1916. They had withstood further German attacks in Champagne as well, but were still not fully recovered from the effects of mutiny. Pétain pressed the British to maintain their pressure on the Germans and Haig was of the opinion that the enemy were close to collapse. Fighting on the Italian front was putting huge demands on their resources, since German units were deployed to bolster the Austro-Hungarian forces there, but Haig resisted demands to send troops from his reserves to support that campaign. In the Salient the French were proving to be invaluable allies. At the opening of Third Ypres they had been relieved at Nieuport by elements of General Sir Henry Rawlinson's Fourth Army and concentrated their efforts alongside the Guards Division to take Bixschoote.

Rawlinson was to advance up the coast when the victory had been achieved in the Salient; he never did. British progress towards Poelcapelle had been satisfactory, but it was on the ridge along which the Menin Road runs that the Germans had held on or regained a significant part of ground lost. Less than two miles had been taken from them.

General Plumer was a methodical man. He had gathered around him a staff of outstanding efficiency, as the smooth running of the Messines Ridge operation had demonstrated. The German tactics of strong counter-attacks by crack units demanded a change of tactics on the British side and Plumer's answer was to limit objectives to what could be taken and held rather than attempt a dramatic breakthrough. To make his preparations he needed three weeks, and during those weeks the pernicious rain eased off. For ten days from 7 September there was almost no rain at all. The ground dried enough to appear virtually normal.

New trenches were dug and roads improved, although not without loss. In this "quiet" period the numbers of killed and wounded continued to mount. In the first two weeks of September more than 10,000 casualties were recorded.

At 5.40am on 20 September what was subsequently called the Battle of the Menin Road Ridge began. The front extended from the meeting of the canal and railway south of Klein Zillebeke to Langemarck in the north of the Salient. The planning of the artillery's part in the battle had been precise. The troops advanced behind a creeping barrage provided by a concentration of guns averaging one to every 5.2 yards. The demonstration of tank power at the Cockcroft appears to have been forgotten. The machines were used in the old style, in support of the infantry, over broken, even if drying, ground. The small contribution they made to the day's events is no surprise. South of the Menin Road the advance was successful in the face of heavy German resistance, but the German strongpoint at Tower Hamlets (J21c, p.73) held out. 123 Brigade had been in reserve and passed through

Below **A corporal, 1st Scots Guards. His rifle is protected by a breech cover, and his steel helmet and leather trench jerkin are strapped to his pack.**
(Osprey, Elite 61, *The Guards 1914-45*)
(Mike Chappell)

124 Brigade, who had secured their objectives, at 8.30am. They threw themselves against Tower Hamlets, but came under heavy fire from the trenches to the south at Bodmin Road. In the afternoon the 23rd Middlesex Regiment, 10th Royal West Kents and the 20th Durham Light Infantry renewed the onslaught across the shallow valley of the Bassevillebeek but Tower Hamlets stood firm.

Along the Menin Road itself the advance swept past Kantinje Cabaret (J21a) to face the next German trench line. The 11th Prince of Wales's Own (West Yorkshire Regiment) and 69 Trench Mortar Battery took the long-time objective of Inverness Copse, though the 9th Yorkshire Regiment (Green Howards – though technically then Alexandra, Princess of Wales's Own), moving up to continue the advance, had a hard time in the smoke and confusion of the battle, suffering casualties from German posts that had been overrun and not mopped up.

What was left of Glencorse Wood, fell to the ANZACs.

What was left of Glencorse Wood, so heavily disputed over the last two months, fell to the ANZACs. The 6th Battalion, 2 (Victoria) Brigade, 1st Australian Division, took it quickly and, to their left, their comrades in the 3 (Queensland) Brigade seized Nonne Bosschen and by 7.45am were in the western edge of Polygon Wood – a remarkable leap forward.

On the approaches to Zonnebeke progress was good. The Zonnebeke Redoubt fell to 27 Brigade and the South Africans took the Bremen Redoubt. To their left the only point of truly stubborn resistance was Schuler Farm (C13a, p.84). The 2/5th Lancashire Fusiliers lost half their men

three days. On 23 September the 12th King's Royal Rifle Corps and the 10th Rifle Brigade renewed the attack. While the German line was subjected to mortar fire, the front being too narrow to risk artillery, the bombing parties made their way forward and began hurling grenades into the trench, working in from either end, as the attack came in with the bayonet. This was successful. All along the line German counter-attacks were rebuffed, many by crushingly accurate artillery fire.

Polygon Wood lies in the elbow of the higher ground, the key to the ridge to the north and Passchendaele. Here the Australians had established themselves in the western fringes, but the bulk of the wood was still held by the Germans. The drive to eject them was to begin on 26 September, but on the day before the Germans had launched a major counter-attack on the line to the north of the Menin Road. The 1st Queen's (Royal West Surrey Regiment) and the 9th

Bombing parties made their way forward and began hurling grenades into the trench.

before taking their part of the strong trench line forward of the farm, Schuler Galleries, and the 1/8th King's Own (Royal Lancaster Regiment) on their left suffered similarly. North and south the line moved forward, but in front of Kansas Cross (D14a, p.84), the focus of Pom and Downing trenches on the Zonnebeke to Langemarck road, a German salient projected into the British gains.

In front of Langemarck, Eagle Trench proved a tough nut to crack. Before they could get at it the 12th Rifle Brigade and the 6th Oxfordshire and Buckinghamshire Light Infantry had the strongpoint of Eagle Farm to deal with, but take it they did and they managed to occupy the southern end of the trench. On their left the 11th Rifle Brigade took severe casualties, losing two-thirds of their men before gaining a section of the trench. Part of it was still in German hands, and remained so for

Highland Light Infantry were forced back, but managed to regain some of the ground with the support of flanking fire from the 2nd Worcesters and the 4th King's (Liverpool Regiment) who had succeeded in holding their positions. The next day, therefore, part of the task became the destruction of the new German positions as well as the subjugation of Polygon Wood. South of the Menin Road, Tower Hamlets fell at last and on the other side of the road to their left 100 Brigade set about the requisition of the previous day's losses. At one point the 1st Queen's were in danger of having their flank turned by a German attack, but two platoons of the 1/9th Highland Light Infantry charged, not only turning the Germans back, but carrying on to regain yet more of the previous day's lost ground. By 4pm they were back on their original line and well enough established to repel

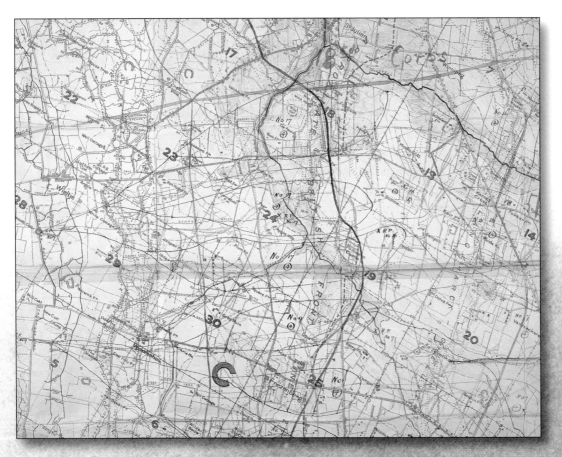

Left **A heavily annotated map of the front between St Julien (top) and Frezenberg (bottom), with German trenches in red and British in black and a superimposed indication of the British front line at 21 August. This is one of two maps in the Tank Museum covered by a note in the same, unknown, hand:** *"One of the 'shows' in the Ypres Salient, about September 1917. I can't remember which this particular one was, but like all the rest taking place there – hopeless!! Reason: See the aeroplane photographs!!"* **(See p.87) The map reproduced here is marked** *"Another forlorn hope!"* Ordnance Survey map Frezenberg 20C. (TM Accn. 22570)

Main picture **Tanks, men and horses at the assembly point at Jackdaw Switch, amid the remains of Sanctuary Wood.** (TM 887/E3)

Right **A captain, 1st Grenadier Guards, his uniform and equipment still sufficiently different in appearance from those of his men to make him easily identified by the enemy as an officer.** (Osprey, Elite 61, *The Guards Divisions 1914–45*) (Mike Chappell)

the inevitable counter-attack. At Black Watch Corner (J15a, p.73) the troops who had held on the day before were to be joined by the 1/4th Suffolk Regiment and the 5/6th Cameronians (Scottish Rifles). The Cameronians came up early in the night and took Jerk House, but the Suffolks were caught in a German barrage just before their start time of 5.15am. Unable to move forward, they lost contact with their own creeping barrage and had to make for Black Watch Corner, well short of their objective.

Such was the enthusiasm with which 15 (Victoria) Brigade, 5th Australian Division, went

into the attack that the 59th Battalion was over-taken by the 29th and 31st who were meant to be in support. The setback suffered by the Suffolks slowed the 31st who came under fire from Cameron House (J16a) and they had to wait until they had re-established contact with them before pushing on. Thus the south-east corner of the wood could not be taken. On their left the advance was more successful. Sergeant J. Stevens of the 58th Battalion (15 [Victoria] Brigade) said:

It was … as though the battalion was carrying out an exercise during manoeuvres.

"A Fokker dived and its machine-gun spat at us. Bock fell."

There were only a few casualties ... Our colonel ... observed that some people were pushing too far forward and we were being caught in our own barrage. So he sent the order forward that we should re-align the position and consolidate it.

The 53rd Australian Battalion (14 [New South Wales] Brigade) stormed and bombed their way to take the Butte, the huge bank that now over-looks the cemetery of that name, and the 55th and 56th came through to reach the eastern side of the wood. The Australian 4th Division smashed their way forward to create a line from the cor-ner of the wood to the brickyard and kiln (D27b, p.96) in Zonnebeke. An Australian stretcher-bear-er, Jim McPhee, was ordered forward from Hell Fire Corner:

Things could not possibly be worse. Up the corduroy track, packed with walking wounded and Hun prisoners from Polygon Wood ... through the horse and mule transport pouring up the cranky, shell-torn road ... On to the Westhoek Ridge, down its slope to Nun's Wood Valley and up the next ridge with earth and smoke spurting. What remained of the tape brought us to some of the 13th Battalion on the crest. The ground appeared to be strewn with dead ... We reached the advanced dressing post pretty exhausted. There the M.O. and dressers of the 15th Battalion coolly dressed outside what wounded wouldn't fit inside. Khaki and grey dead looked up ... Three squads shoul-dered stretchers in good heart till we struck a worse belt of fury, the stetcher wob-bled, and we stumbled. A Fokker dived and its machine-gun spat at us. Bock fell. We examined him and decided to return later to bury him and the patient ... A Hun took Bock's place for a carry and we worked quickly till nightfall ... a deeper gloom, through which we blundered into entanglements and cursed. A bearer stepped into a shell hole and down the wounded man top-pled into the foul mud. A great radiance flamed red in the sky above Ypres.

Above **Nonne Bosschen –
Nun's Wood – taken by
3 Australian Brigade on 20
September. The row of
pillboxes was photographed
on 1 October.** (IWM E(AUS).870)

Below **Tanks squandered in
impossible conditions near
Veldhoek, photographed the
day after the attack of 20
September.** (TM 1577/B3)

We made it. We advanced about a mile, thanks to the mist. The trouble was we couldn't find this mill. I could see this patch of water and I said, "Well, that must be Zonnebeke Lake and that must be the church, what's left of it" – for it was just a pile of rubble – "but I can't see the windmill." And then as I was looking round I saw a faint trace of a track with some white rubble at the end of the track, and that was it. That was "Le Moulin"… We had no trouble, just the usual fighting, and we also had a shrapnel barrage … You could see the flash going in front of us and it was very accurate … It was so easy that some people got wounded, because they went on so fast into our own barrage and through it.

Alongside the Australians on 26 September the 2nd Suffolk Regiment were overlooking Zonnebeke Lake. They had moved forward with the 10th Royal Welsh Fusiliers on their left and, after finding a way across the bog that had been the little Zonnebeek stream, came under machine-gun fire from the railway station. This strongpoint held out so that the eventual line kinked back from the western side of the village before turning north to Hill 40 (D21d), which the 2nd Royal Scots and the 7th King's Shropshire Light Infantry had reached but not taken. Acting Captain L. J. Baker of the 2nd Suffolks said of that day:

The blockhouses around Kansas Cross had withstood the attacks of August, but they fell this day to the four battalions of the Sherwood Foresters of 178 Brigade (59th Division). At the end of the day a serious gap still existed on the southern flank of the Australians in Polygon Wood, but the strongpoint of Cameron House was reported taken at 5.40am the next day, and 98 and 100 Brigades (33rd Division) thrust forward to complete the line. After three days of comparative quiet this sector suffered ferocious German counter-attacks and Cameron House

"It was a terrible strain to lie there under that sort of fire without being able to do a thing about it ..."

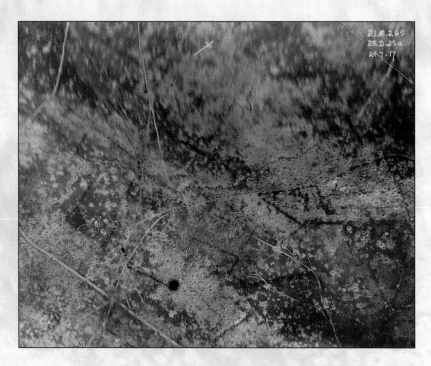

lie there under that sort of fire without being able to do a thing about it ...

Above **Close comparison of this photograph with square D25a on the map on p.84 will show that the crossroads on the left are at Frezenberg. The cross symbol points north, as do the grid lines on the map. The picture was taken on 27 July, by which time the terrain has already been pulverised by the artillery, while some trenches so clearly marked on the map have all but disappeared.**
(TM 5410/A4)

was lost, only to be retaken by the 9th Leicestershire Regiment.

On 2 October it rained, and the next day. It was to rain almost every day until the end of the month. It seemed to be ordained that during preparations for battle the weather should be fine and that as soon as movement became vital to survival the rain fell. The ploughed and shattered earth soaked it up and the emerging trackways were once more reduced to quagmire. Most important of all, it became almost impossible to move the guns which had served so well to provide covering bombardments for troops moving forward and to break up concentrations of German troops preparing to counter-attack.

A German attack was, at that moment, assembling. Their front line above Zonnebeke and facing Polygon Wood was thronged with troops ready to go forward after the morning bombardment of 3 October. The British and Australians were similarly poised to go into action, though without a preliminary bombardment, and when the German guns opened up the men were caught in the maelstrom. The Australians, 2 Brigade (1st Division), were south of Zonnebeke Lake. W. J. Harvey was getting his rum ration when the shells began to fall.

They pounded our positions with high explosives, including minenwerfers and eight-inch shells, and we had tremendous casualties ... We had forty killed, including two of our platoon officers, and taking into account the wounded a third of our men were put out of action. Everyone kept their nerve, although it was a terrible strain to

Minutes later the British barrage began and the Australians charged the German line. The surprise was complete; those Germans who could, fled, leaving the rest to be killed by the bayonet or taken prisoner. Four field guns being used as anti-tank weapons were overrun and the Australians swept up the steep slope to take Broodseinde Ridge (D29c, p.96). On their right the 1st Division's 8th Battalion was forced into the 2nd Australian Division's sector by having to avoid the floods in the valley and by a number of pillboxes, the destruction of which drew them off their line, but they too gained the ridge. They came under fire from four 77mm guns on the Becelaere-Broodseinde road and punished this impertinence by capturing the weapons.

North-east of Polygon Wood the attack went equally well alongside the Australians, with the 2nd Gordon Highlanders, the 8th Devonshire Regiment and the 2nd Border Regiment also reaching the objective. Further south, where the ridge road bends away south-eastwards at Jay Cottage, the 22nd Manchester Regiment came under fire from Joiner's Rest and had to be reinforced by the 21st Manchesters before they could make their ground. To their right there was trouble, the advance lagging behind, and they were obliged to form a south-facing flank to cover the front of 62 Brigade (21st Division). East of Polygon Wood the land falls gently away to the south-east and the shallow valley of the Reutelbeek beyond which stands, or at the time lay, Gheluvelt. The renewed rain and the continuing shellfire had the expected results.

Acting Captain Clement Robertson of A Battalion, Tank Corps knew he had to get his machines across the Reutelbeek to deal with pill-boxes that would threaten the infantry. He and his servant spent three days scouting out the ground and marking with tape the route to be followed. There was constant shellfire all the while. Then, on foot, he led his tanks as the attack developed, guided them to the bridge and set them on their way. Inevitably German artillery fire was brought down on the lumbering machines, and with equal inevitability Robertson was killed. He was awarded a posthumous VC and his servant the DCM.

When the 9th King's Own Yorkshire Light Infantry advanced they came under machine-gun fire from a number of pill-boxes, which they

The British were elated. But what to do next? The rain just went on and on.

Main picture **A mule train brings up supplies in preparation for the attack of 26 September, passing a tank stuck on a tree-stump at Clapham Junction.** (TM 1510/C4)

dealt with, but then they ran into extremely dangerous fire from a strongpoint on the east of Reutel. It was silenced by a tank of A Battalion.

Over the difficult ground before Gheluvelt on the southern flank of the action there was poor progress. The Germans counter-attacked in strength and, from no forward movement for heavy loss south of Tower Hamlets, through a modest advance between the Menin Road and Polygon Wood, to a stunning success on Broodseinde Ridge, the results varied. North of Zonnebeke the Australians had advanced to take a line from Broodseinde village northwards, running down the slope to Tyne Cot (D17a), where the New Zealanders were on their flank. They had taken the Abraham Heights (D15b) and pushed beyond Gravenstafel as far as Waterloo (D9d), overlooking the Ravebeek which flows west from Passchendaele into a confusion of channels to emerge as the Stroombeek. To the north Poelcapelle had been taken at last by elements of 34 and 33 Brigades, the 11th Manchester Regiment and the 7th South Staffordshire Regiment working with tanks of D Battalion, Tank Corps. As the day wore on the rain increased to a full storm. Counter-attacks died away, but so did any further advance. The shell-holes filled anew.

The Germans were deeply dissatisfied with the day's work, and Crown Prince Rupprecht's Chief of Staff observed "[he] found himself compelled to consider whether … he should not withdraw the front in Flanders so far back that the Allies would be forced to carry out an entirely new deployment of artillery." The British were elated. But what to do next? The rain just went on and on. Over the next four days more than an inch (30mm) fell on the sodden Salient. Gough and Plumer proposed to suspend attacks, but Haig could see the prize of Passchendaele within his grasp. Only the centre of the ridge was theirs – and surely one more thrust would give them command of the whole? Besides, one could scarcely stop here: the position was untenable as a defensive line against the Germans

Above **A lance-corporal of 126 Brigade's (42nd Division) Light Trench Mortar Battery with a Stokes mortar fitted with handles and sling for mobile use.** (Osprey, MAA 245, *British Territorial Units 1914-18*) (Mike Chappell)

"The duckboards were being blown up and men being blown off the track or simply slipping off."

and it would be necessary to fall back. How could that be explained to the politicians and the public at home? Had all the effort since 31 July been futile? They would go on.

More troops moved up in anticipation of the attack of 9 October. The 2/5th East Lancashire Regiment were to be the support in 198 Brigade's advance through Tyne Cot. Lieutenant P. King described the horrors of the march up from Ypres.

It was an absolute nightmare. Often we would have to stop and wait for up to half an hour, because all the time the duck-boards were being blown up and men being blown off the track or simply slipping off – because we were all in full marching order with gas-masks and rifles, and some were carrying machine-guns and extra ammunition.

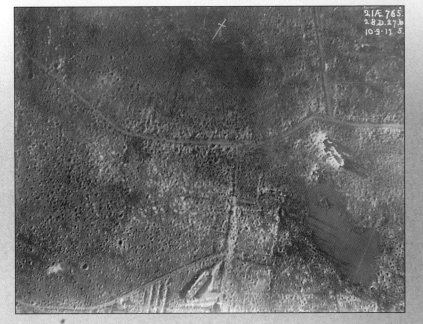

At 5.20am on 9 October the 2/9th Manchester Regiment and the 2/4th East Lancashires (both 198 Brigade, 66th Division) advanced against Dab Trench (D16b). Fire from Hamburg Redoubt, the

"We could hardly move because the mud was so heavy that you were dragging your legs behind you."

strongpoint in the centre of the obstacle, cut the men down and an attempt by the 2/5th East Lancashires to take it failed. Some of them never even saw it, as King described.

We went over into this morass, straight into a curtain of rain and mist and shells, for we were caught between the two barrages. Well, of course, we lost direction right away … The machine-gun fire from the German positions was frightful … We could hardly move because the mud was so heavy that you were dragging your legs behind you, and with people being hit and falling and splashing down all round you, all you can do is keep moving and look for some form of cover.

King and his surviving men were pinned down in a shell-hole for 24 hours. As evening fell the next day, he was surprised by voices behind him and turned to see three tall men, casually smoking. He asked who they were and told them to douse their cigarettes for fear of drawing enemy fire. The reply came, "Well, we're the Aussies, chum, and we've come to relieve you."

Up on the ridge 6 Australian Brigade fought their line east to take Daisy Wood and Dairy Wood while 5 Brigade pushed north along the ridge. They got as far as the road and railway crossing, Defy Crossing, but the men in the mud-bath before Tyne Cot were struggling, leaving the German machine-guns free to turn their fire on the ridge. The advance halted. The 1st Australian Division were holding the southern flank of the attacking line, but also undertook an attack on the strongly held German positions in Celtic Wood. The force of 85 men went in with vigour. Of those 14 returned; what became of the others is, to this day, unknown.

North of the Langemarck–Poelcapelle road the 4th, 29th and Guards Divisions were thrusting up towards the Houthulst Forest, beyond which the northern end of the Passchendaele Ridge could be outflanked. The 11th Division had been

stopped by the blockhouses in their effort to advance east from Poelcapelle, and this exposed the right flank of the 4th's 12 Brigade, limiting what they could achieve. On their left the 2nd Royal Fusiliers, Ernest Parker with them, was in support of the 1st Lancashire Fusiliers. Before the attack, in the dark and rain, disorientated by the lack of identifiable features in the blasted landscape, he had difficulty in finding the correct position from which they were meant to start and wandered around, shell fragments rattling off his helmet, until he discovered where he should be. He returned to his platoon to move them off.

As they climbed out of their shell holes our preliminary bombardment opened up with the crushing violence of a thunderstorm. At the same time day began to break and from all points of the compass the shining bayonets of the attack thrust themselves from innumerable holes in the earth. The men of the 2nd Royals in long files of platoons began their advance towards the enemy, cut off from sight by a long wall of smoke rising from the shells of the creeping barrage ... On reaching some higher ground I had a good view over the top of the barrage, and a mile away could be seen the edges of the Houthulst Forest, towards which a long straight line of men moved as if on parade. These were the Guards, and I thought that if they were covering ground similar to ours their great prestige was

Above **The 5th Australian Division Memorial stands over Buttes New British Cemetery in Polygon Wood, facing the New Zealand Memorial to the Missing. The Butte on which it stands was an isolated heap of earth in a bare landscape when the Australians took it in September 1917.**
(DP)

Left **German prisoners carry a wounded man past entrenched British troops.**
(IFF)

well deserved. **Our people were either advancing in small knots, or, like my own platoon, strung out in crocodile formation. When the barrage halted we all jumped into shell holes.**

Parker moved about to sort out the platoon, but was immediately shot through the wrist. It was the end of his war – a "blighty one". The brigade went on to take its objectives and on their left was the Royal Newfoundland Regiment (88 Brigade, 29th Division), men of the then separate colony off the Canadian coast. Between the road and the railway, they made good progress until held up by fire from a blockhouse in front of Namur Crossing. They were waiting for mortars to be brought up when the firing suddenly ceased. Private Dancox

had silenced it single-handed. The delay led to a slight kink in the final line round Egypt Farm where the Guards, who had taken all their objectives with a steady inevitability against a stubborn enemy, had to make allowance for the slight shortfall of the Newfoundlanders' advance. On the Guards' left the French waded through the mud that had once been the Broembeek to take Mangelaere and Veldhoek, reaching the south-western edge of the Houthulst Forest.

The fate of the wounded was uncertain. Some walked or crawled through the slime to dressing stations, some were retrieved by stretcher-bearers. Some crouched or lay in shell-holes filled with water and, below the water, mud. Sergeant T. Berry of the 1st Rifle Brigade saw what happened to them

We heard screaming coming from another crater a bit away ... It was a big hole and there was this fellow of the 8th Suffolks in it up to his shoulders. So

Right **A lance-bombardier (artillery equivalent of a lance-corporal), Royal Field Artillery. He wears the groundsheet/cape, waterproof and the small box respirator introduced in 1917. His carrying panniers hold the black shrapnel and yellow high explosive (HE) rounds for an 18-pounder field gun. The overseas service stripes on his sleeve were introduced in 1918.**

(Osprey, MAA 182, *British Battle Insignia 1914–18*)   (Mike Chappell)

Below right **A wounded man is lifted from a tank to a Ford ambulance at St Julien, 27 September.** (TM 202/B6)

> # "He kept begging us to shoot him. But we couldn't shoot him. Who could shoot him?"

I said, "Get your rifles, one man in the middle to stretch them out, make a chain and let him get hold of it." But it was no use. It was too far … The more we pulled and the more he struggled the further he seemed to go down. He went down gradually. He kept begging us to shoot him. But we couldn't shoot him. Who could shoot him? We stayed with him, watching him go down in the mud. And he died.

In the north the British seemed well placed, and, right of centre, on the Broodseinde Ridge, the Australians were solidly established, but between the two men were mired down where once little streams had flowed, while further south, in front of Gheluvelt, the irresistible force had met the immovable object. Further afield new pressures on the Allies were mounting. Intelligence reported the massing of 42 divisions of the Central Powers on the Italian front and the demand for reinforcements from the BEF gained in urgency. In Russia the Kerensky government (established after the Revolution in March, but now threatened by Lenin's Bolsheviks) was tottering, making the movement of German divisions from the Eastern to the Western Front

likely in the immediate future. There seemed so little a distance yet to go to secure Passchendaele, though the rain fell without cease. Haig was determined to continue. Gough asked Plumer to cancel the attack. He declined.

The axis of the attack of 12 October was on a line running north-east from the waterlogged approaches to the ridge from Tyne Cot to Poelcapelle, with the ANZACs at the south and the British on the north. The German line was under significantly reduced pressure from artillery. Where it was possible to shell their line, and the foul weather ruled out spotting by aircraft, the shells buried themselves deep in the ooze, throwing up splendid showers of mud but doing little to smash the wire or damage the pill-boxes. Getting the guns up at all to cover the attack was an almost insurmountable challenge. Gunner B. O. Stokes of 13 Battery, New Zealand Field Artillery recalled:

C and D guns went forward first, and didn't they have a time getting them through the sea of mud and slush! They had to have eight horse-teams to do the job … We only managed to get four guns out of our six-gun battery forward …

The men gathering for the attack had to suffer the foul conditions, for there was no alternative. Private W. Smith of 2 New Zealand Machine Gun Company:

It was a terrible night. We dug in as best we could at the bottom of the Bellevue Ridge – but the idea of "digging in" was ridiculous. You can't dig water! My section managed to throw up a ridge of slush, but the water from the shell-holes around just poured into it. You couldn't squat down, we just stood there in the rain and wind waiting for our guns to open up with the barrage.

Up on the ridge the 4th Australian Division attempted to push along the road to Passchendaele, but could achieve little as the 3rd Division on their left was even harder pressed by German resistance. They suffered severe losses for minimal gain. On their left the 3rd Division's 34th Battalion was shattered by shellfire as they attempted to move off, but the 35th, in support, were, if the term can be used at all in such circumstances, luckier. They managed to overrun Augustus Wood (D11c) and some of them even contrived to get up on to the ridge, where they found isolated groups of the 66th British Division still clinging on from the attack of 9 September.

A few even got as far as the village of Passchendaele itself, but not in sufficient strength to remain there. Further to the left the 40th Battalion took Waterfields (D10d) but could go no further in the face of machine-gun fire from Bellevue (D4d).

The New Zealanders, advancing from Waterloo (D9d), were fearfully mauled. The wire on the Gravenstafel road was uncut and covered by pillboxes. None the less the 2nd Otago Regiment (2 NZ Brigade, New Zealand Division)

Above **At the north of the Salient Belgian troops shelter as best they can in the rain and mud.** (PBC-Brugge 271/10)

Below **Troops move forward on duckboards weaving through the mud and shell holes near Albania Woods, 12 October.** (IWM E(AUS).985)

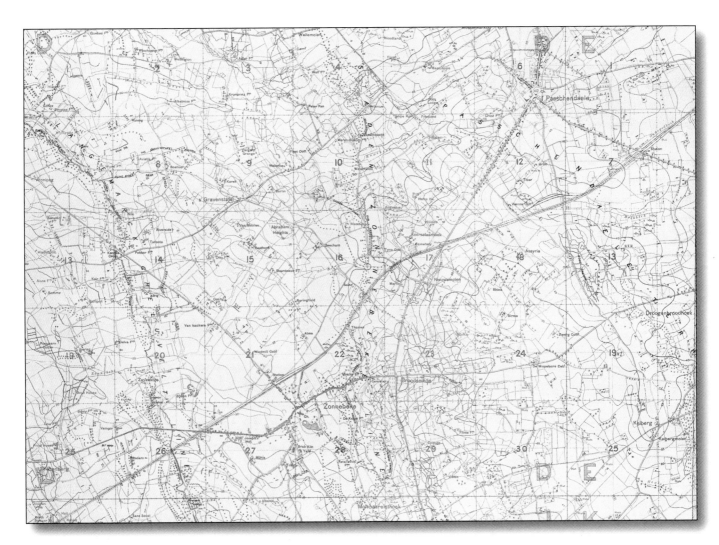

got up to the wire where there was a small gap on the road, only to be cut down by machine-gun fire. The 1st Otagos (1 NZ Brigade) attempted to help, even trying to crawl under the wire. It was hopeless. Private W. Smith once more:

We made a bad "blue" in sticking to that main Passchendaele road. It certainly looked the best part to get a footing on – covered with inches of mud, of course, but with a fairly firm footing underneath … As we started up the road we were being caught in enfilade fire from the big pill-boxes in the low ground to our right. People were dropping all the way. Then, as we turned the corner on top of the rise, we saw this great bank of wire ahead, maybe a hundred yards away. A rat couldn't have

got through that. The bombardment should have cut the wire but it hadn't even dented it. Not that we could get near it anyway, for it was positively spitting fire.

The only strongpoint taken was further to the left where, together with elements of the 9th (Scottish) Division, the New Zealanders added the Cemetery (D4a) and Wolf Farm (D4c) to the puny gains of the day.

Further north the attacks met with equally poor results. The Guards prodded into the edge of the Houthulst Forest with little to show for it and the attempt against Poelcapelle by the 18th (Eastern) Division managed to reach no further than the east side of the village. A brief flurry of action ten days later, on 22 October, in front of Poelcapelle brought only the Brewery (20a, p. 101),

Above **The three major lines of German defence in front of Passchendaele, with German trenches in red and British in blue, corrected to 8 September 1917.** Ordnance Survey map Zonnebeke, 28NE1, Ed.7A. (IFF)

Right **A detail from a German map of the defence lines west of Passchendaele ridge. The road running diagonally across the top of the map is from Waterloo to Bellevue (D4d) to Mosselmarkt and the road down the map leads to Tyne Cot.** (BH)

which was taken by the 8th Norfolk Regiment, and Meunier House (20b, p.101) which fell to the 10th Essex Regiment.

That was the First Battle of Passchendaele, and it had brought virtually no gain on the ground and massive losses in men. The British were almost used up. The ANZACs had been squandered. It was the case that the Germans had sent 12 divisions, destined for Italy from the Eastern Front, to the Ypres Salient instead, but that was the limit to any claim of success.

It was decided to suspend operations in the hope of better weather, and true to form, the rain let up a little. Haig still had some superb troops available and any new move would wait on the weather and on the men – the Canadians.

The Canadians returned to the Ypres Salient on 18 October, under a new commander, a Canadian, Lieutenant-General Sir Arthur Currie, as he had by now become. They could hardly

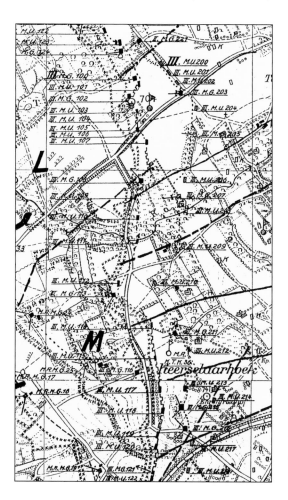

Above right **The meadows in front of Tyne Cot became a marsh that would have been dangerous enough even without bullets and shells to worry about. The largest Commonwealth War Graves Commission cemetery in the world is now here, with 11,908 graves and the names of 34,984 missing carved on the curving wall. German pillboxes remain here, and one carries a memorial to the 2nd Australian Division which took Tyne Cot Blockhouse on 4 October 1917.** (MFME Ypres 2.12)

Below right **From the 7th Division Memorial, south of Broodseinde, Mount Kemmel is clearly visible ten miles away, emphasising the importance of the ridge to an occupying army. The 2nd Australian Division took this position on 4 October.**
(MFME Yp/Ar 3/20)

recognise the ground. The villages they had known were all gone, the woods had disappeared, the streams were now broad bogs. Only the faint trace of the roads to Zonnebeke and Gravenstafel served as reference points in the blighted landscape. They took over the line from the Zonnebeke road in the south to a point astride the Gravenstafel-Mosselmarkt road, the sector of the last great ANZAC attack. A huge effort was at once undertaken to build roads and tracks to get

Above **Troops supposedly resting out of the line in fact got little repose. These Australian soldiers are collecting rubble to repair the shattered roads, 1 November 1917.** (IWM E(AUS).1403)

Below **Australian transport on the Menin Road, screened to provide some cover from the eyes of German observers, 23 October 1917.** (IWM E(AUS).1391)

guns and supplies forward. Their work was hampered by continual shelling and by the introduction of a new gas by the Germans, diphenyl chlorarsine, "Blue Cross", which penetrated the current design of gas-mask and caused uncontrollable sneezing and vomiting.

The Germans had been rethinking their defensive tactics. The British approach of leap-frogging their units, one consolidating as the next passed through, behind a creeping barrage which made any German counter-attack so costly, had worked well at Menin Road Ridge and Polygon

Wood against the German scheme of lightly defended front lines. A heavily defended front line had failed at Broodseinde. The concept of the "forefield" was now introduced in which the lightly defended front line would be separated from the main defensive positions by as much as 500 to 1,000 metres, the intervening ground to be saturated with artillery fire as soon as the outposts had been withdrawn. The three regiments of the 11th Bavarian Division on the Passchendaele Ridge each had one battalion in the main defensive position with the remaining two in successive lines to the rear, awaiting the Canadian attack (See map, p.101).

The German front was plastered with shellfire for four days along its whole length. Particular attention paid to pillboxes and blockhouses on the intended line of attack was disguised by equal fury falling elsewhere. General Currie attempted to solve the problem of the Ravebeek bog by leaving it alone, a decision which certainly prevented useless casualties.

At 5.40am on 26 October the Second Battle of Passchendaele began. On either side of the Menin Road the British 7th and 5th Divisions were frustrated by the marshes that now protected Gheluvelt. Along the ridge and across the Broodseinde-Passchendaele road the 46th Canadian Battalion, with the 18th Australian

Battalion on their right, went forward in a mist that, as the day drew on, turned to steady rain. They took their objectives, but the Canadians paid heavily with 70 per cent casualties. It was a mistake to allocate this sector to two different formations as confusion was inevitable. Decline Copse (D18a, p.96), straddling the railway, was reported as taken by both Canadians and Australians. Each therefore withdrew to leave it to the other and the Germans moved back in. They were not ejected for another 24 hours, after a night attack by the 44th Canadian Battalion.

Against the Bellevue Ridge (D4d) the 43rd Battalion from 9 Canadian Brigade made good progress, clearing the pillboxes with grenades, but on their right the 58th were checked by the Laamkeek blockhouse. From the hill above, the Germans were able to direct a telling shellfire on the attackers, and they were forced to fall back, but some of them held on. Lieutenant Robert Shankland of the 43rd with the added strength of men of 9 Machine Gun Company clung on to a position on the Bellevue Spur, occupying the former German positions. By noon the 52nd had come up in support to reunite the outpost with the brigade and went on to secure the rest of the spur. They took the pillboxes one by one, rifle grenades providing cover while small parties of soldiers crept their way round to hurl hand

grenades through the loopholes. It was tough, dirty work, but by evening defences that had repelled the British and the New Zealanders were secured. Robert Shankland was awarded the VC. To their left the 63rd (Royal Naval) Division had gained some ground but, just as down on the Menin Road, anything other than a hill was now a lake. The Canadians, at least, had two hand-holds on higher ground.

In the dark the work of finding and tending the wounded went on. Private F. Hodgson of the 11th Canadian Field Ambulance, was at Tyne Cot.

Above **A corduroy road at Idiot Corner, Westhoek Ridge; Australian soldiers and supplies moving towards the front line, 5 November 1917.** (IWM E(AUS).1480)

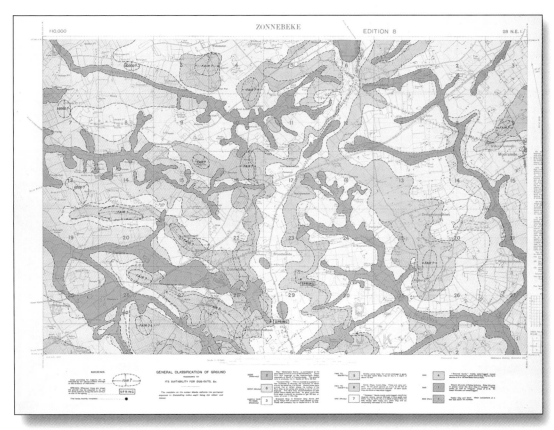

ZONNEBEKE   EDITION 8   28 N.E.I.

GENERAL CLASSIFICATION OF GROUND

Left **This Ordnance Survey General Classification of Ground map is dated November 1917. The data on which it is based must clearly have been available a significant time before publication. The solid line of the Passchendaele Ridge runs up the centre, surrounded by the blue shading indicating waterlogged and mostly waterlogged ground. Ignorance of the conditions cannot, therefore, be admitted as an explanation for decisions of the High Command.** Ordnance Survey map Zonnebeke 28NE1. (IFF)

Below **The field of Passchendaele after the battle. Even this desolate scene only hints at the conditions endured by the Canadians.** (IWM C.O.2264)

Right **A map of the terrain forward of Poelcapelle, based on the edition corrected to 6 July, and corrected and added to by an unknown British hand.** Ordnance Survey 20SE3, VW. (TM)

We had two pillboxes there ... the doctor and his helpers were in one and we stretcher-bearers were in another about a hundred feet away ... There were three squads of us. Three squads of eight – because it took six of us at a time to get one stretcher out through the mud. That day we drew lots to see who should go first. My squad drew the last carry ... Away we went with our wounded man, struggling down the track. After a few hundred yards we were caught in a barrage. We put the stretcher-case in a depression on the ground. He was very frightened, the wounded boy ... He died before we could get him to the dressing station. On the way back we passed the remains of our No. 1 Squad. There was nothing but limbs all over the place. We lost ten of our stretcher-bearers that day.

The Canadians had lost 2,481 men over the three days of their first strike at Passchendaele, of whom 585 were killed. Currie declined to rush into further attacks and three more days passed as roads were repaired and fresh preparations made. On 30 October the assault began again. The German reply to the artillery barrage did not come for eight precious minutes by which time the Canadians were well on the move. On the right the 85th Battalion (12 Brigade, 4th Canadian Division) took Vienna Cottage (D12c) and reached its final objective but lost half its men in doing so, and to their left the 78th were over-looking the eastern slope of the ridge. The 72nd, also, like the 78th, one of 12 Brigade's battalions, were heading for Crest Farm (D12a), moving along the side of the ridge and fanning out to the left to take it. Their forward patrols found the Germans preparing to retreat from Passchendaele village. Below them the Ravebeek was flooded, limiting their ability to establish a secure line, and beyond it Princess Patricia's Canadian Light Infantry (& Brigade, 3rd Canadian Division) were having a tough time, so the final line established curled back from Crest Farm. Private J. Pickard of the 78th was a signaller, but the shellfire destroyed telephone cable as fast as it could be laid, so he became a runner.

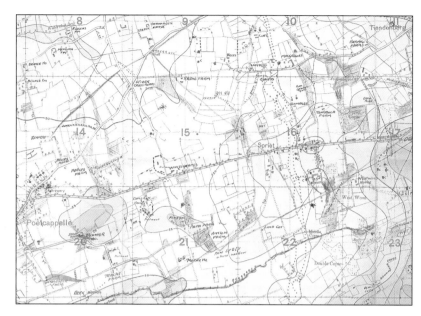

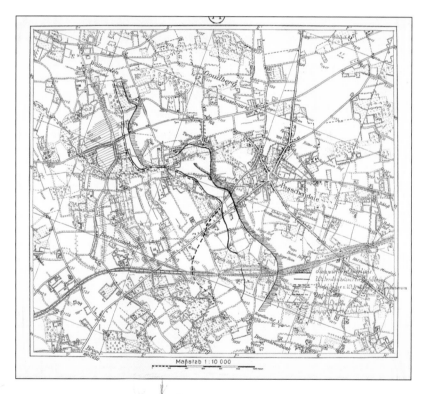

Right **German and Canadian positions west of Passchendaele corrected to 20 October 1917, from the map of the 11th Bavarian Division. The solid blue line with hatching marks the main line of German defence, the plain blue line the forefield defence and the blue dashes the forefield itself, which coincides with the forefield defence in some places. The solid red line shows the British line and the red hatching the trench works. The place names on the British map (p.96) relate to this map as follows: Graf (D5d) = Turm Hof; Duck Lodge (d5c) = West Hof; Crest Farm (D12a) is at co-ordinate 1346; Vienna Cottage (D12c) = Stein Hof. Ehrenfriedhof is a cemetery such as the one to the east of Tyne Cot (D17A.**
(BH, 11.Inf.Div.Bd.23, Akt6.)

Right **The Canadian Memorial in the village of Passendale today.** (MFME Yp/Ar 3/18)

The Germans were surprised before they could man their machine-guns

It started to rain in the afternoon, but it went well that day. I was back and forward to the line as acting-runner, and every time we'd got a bit nearer to Passchendaele. They stopped eventually at the foot of a lane leading into the village. You could tell it had been a lane by the ruined cottages on either side, and you could see the church just beyond them. It was a place they called Crest Farm. They had to fight hard to get it and the place was thick with bodies. But we took it, and we held the line.

The PPCLI had to work their way through the strongpoints of Snipe Hall (D11a), which they took at night before the attack in a surprise move, and Duck Lodge (D5c) before they could seize the Meetcheele crossroads (D5b) under heavy fire, and there they dug in, well up the Bellevue Spur and an obvious threat to the German possession of the ridge. They nearly did not make it. A pillbox beside the road had them under a punishing fire and two men tackled it. Lieutenant Hugh Mackenzie drew their fire, and died doing so, while Sergeant George Mullin worked his way round to attack the post alone, killing the two machine-gunners with his revolver. Both men were awarded the VC. Below the spur to the left the 5th Canadian Mounted Rifles (8 Brigade, 3rd Canadian Division) struggled through the swamp of Woodland Plantation (D5a) and by mid-after-

noon they were well up the ridge. The third Canadian VC of the day was won here when Major George Pearkes held Vapour Farm and Source Farm against German counter-attacks. Graf House (D5d) was still holding out. The action had proved as costly to the Canadians in a single day as the previous three-day attack: 884 killed and 1,429 wounded. To the Canadian left a disaster attended the opening of the attack when the Royal Naval Division's 190 Brigade was caught by a German counter-barrage. The surviving troops could achieve little.

German counter-attacks over the next few days were determined and frequent, but largely unsuccessful. Currie took a seven-day break before the next operation. The 3rd and 4th Canadian Divisions were relieved by the 1st and 2nd Divisions and preparations were made for the next thrust. It came on 6 November, with the rest of Plumer's force raising a ruckus on the flanks, but leaving the hard fighting to the Canadians. On the heels of the barrage that broke over the Germans at 6am the 27th Battalion (6 Brigade, 2nd Canadian Division) moved forward with such speed that the Germans were surprised before they could man their machine-guns in front of Passchendaele, and by 8.45am the village was in Canadian hands. At the northern end the pillboxes offered a firm resistance, but the 27th and 31st soon put an end to that. On their left the other battalion of 6 Brigade, the 28th, starting from the boggy depths of the Ravebeek which was, according to the brigade report, knee-deep and in places waist-deep in mud and water, came under heavy fire. On the other side of the bog, on the Bellevue Spur, the 1st and 2nd Battalions (1 Brigade, 1st Canadian Division) took the garrison of the blockhouse at Mosselmarkt (D6a) by surprise and 54 men surrendered without a fight. The surrounding shell-holes were filled with Germans who did not give in so easily, but by 8am they had been overcome. On the extreme left, beyond the bog that had been a tributary of the Lekkerboterbeek, the 3rd Battalion ran into fierce fire from Vine Cottages. Corporal Colin Barron won the VC for

Corporal Colin Barron won the VC for rushing the strongpoint and capturing three machine-gun posts

rushing the strongpoint and capturing three machine-gun posts, using one of their own guns to put the defenders to flight. The action was swift, decisive and costly. Casualties amounted to 2,238, of whom 734 were killed or died of wounds.

In a final effort in torrential rain four days later, on 10 November, the line was pushed to the north, the Canadians fighting alongside the British, with the latter's 3 Brigade, 1st Division on their left. A barrage drove the 1st South Wales Borderers and the 2nd Royal Munster Fusiliers apart and a German counter-attack exploited the gap. The Canadians (2 and 4 Brigades of the 1st Division), meanwhile, had pushed up the road towards Vindictive Crossroads and had to fall back on the left to maintain contact with the retiring 3 Brigade. The final position was a vulnerable salient above Passchendaele which the Germans pounded unmercifully over the next four days, although the Canadians did succeed in pushing forward down the eastern side of the ridge to make the position more secure. On 14 November their relief commenced. On 15 November the Third Battle of Ypres was declared over.

The losses on both sides had been huge and,

as is usual in controversial circumstances, have been disputed over the years. The likely total figures for all casualties (killed, wounded, missing or made prisoner) are 244,897 British (including Dominion and Empire forces), 8,525 French and approximately 230,000 German. The whole episode has been condemned as futile by some; while, with more justification, continuing the assault after the successes of late September has been branded as criminal. It appears that, right or wrong as he might have been, Haig was genuinely convinced that the Germans were on the point of breaking by the end of September. His concept of crushing the Germans in Flanders, securing the Channel coast and then turning south to roll up the German line was imaginative and viable, but depended entirely on the success of the first phase in the Ypres Salient. It is also the case that the Germans themselves viewed their losses as a calamity, seriously undermining their ability to win the war, and where they had no further reserves of manpower to call on, the Allies could look to America. Whatever the arguments, however, what cannot be disputed is the courage and endurance of those who fought at Ypres.

1918:
THE LAST BATTLES

Below **British troops in dugouts near Zillebeke, 15 February 1918. A tank awaits a recovery team.** (TM 866/B5)

O n 24 October the Central Powers unleashed an overwhelming attack on the Italian front at Caporetto, and within days the Italian Army was in retreat on a broad front across the north-east of their country. Almost immediately two British divisions were dispatched to Italy from the Western Front, and within a fortnight General Plumer was in Mantua as Commander-in-Chief of the British forces. His reorganisation of the Allied forces was to save the situation. In Flanders General Rawlinson took over. In mid-November the Bolshevik Revolution took Russia, in effect, out of the war, although no formal ceasefire would be agreed for some time. On the Western Front another revolution was demonstrated: the way in which tanks could

"Hell itself would be nice and peaceful."

change the conduct of warfare. The Battle of Cambrai, in which the British tanks broke through the Hindenburg Line, ended in stalemate, but the principle of using the machines over sound ground to spearhead attacks on prepared positions was clear at last.

In the Ypres Salient the front line was now separated from its supply of men and matériel by a wilderness. George Ashurst was serving with the 16th Lancashire Fusiliers and arrived in the Salient from Nieuport in November 1917.

As far as the eye could see the land was honeycombed; different tracks to the front line could be picked out by the slippery duck-boards zigzagging along the edge of the muddy craters ... Lying about were wrecked gun carriages and ration carts. Aeroplanes lay where they had fallen ... Pieces of equipment, damaged tin hats, bully beef tins, jam tins, broken rifles and rusty bayonets, barbed wire and wiring stakes were strewn about in the grey mud, one long desolate waste as far as the eye could see, to the ridge in the far distance where at intervals a dirty black smoke rose from the earth mingled with countless lumps of dirt, and where tin-hatted grimy men pulled at dried fag-ends and uttered curses and wishes not to be written. Hell itself would be nice and peaceful compared with Passchendaele.

It was, once again, quiet on this front. Just the routine shelling and sniping, rain and snow, wounding and killing.

In March 1918 Ludendorff put his last great plan into action. He was able to withdraw half a million men from the Eastern Front to support the effort. By attacking without a long bombardment, thereby achieving surprise, and using specially trained storm troops he would smash through the Allied lines and turn his opponents' flanks. The frequency and ferocity of trench raids was increased, and though the Allies were aware of the overall purpose, they could not know

where Ludendorff would strike. The first great attack, Operation Michael, fell on the junction of the French and the British Armies on the Somme. The line was thinly held, not only because of the transfer of troops to Italy, but also because of the unwillingness of senior British politicians to supply Haig with more men to be used up in repeats of the Somme and of Passchendaele. The March offensive swept the Allies back almost to Amiens with the loss of a quarter of a million men, nearly half of them made prisoner, but there it ran out of energy and halted, largely of its own accord. The supply lines were overstretched and many of the best soldiers that Germany could put in the field were dead or wounded.

On 9 April the next blow fell in Operation Georgette, an attack between Armentières and Béthune, on the River Lys west of Lille. General Plumer had returned on 17 March from Italy to command the Second Army again; now he found

Left **A tank rigged as a mobile crane salvaging parts from a derelict machine. Two men of the Chinese Labour Corps look on. Some 100,000 Chinese recruited from coastal regions around Hong Kong and other European enclaves were serving in support of the BEF by the end of the war. Tank Corps Central Stores, Erin, near St Pol, 10 February 1918.** (TM 5410/B6)
Below **German assault troops. From left to right: NCO, Bavarian assault battalion; NCO, 5th Stürmbataillon "Rohr"; assault infantryman; private, Assault Company, 23rd Saxon (1st Saxon) Reserve Division.** (Osprey, MAA 80, *The German Army 1914-18*) (Gerry Embleton)

Right **German storm troopers advancing with the support of a captured tank, now marked with German insignia.**
(TM 2412/B5)

Main picture **Mobile warfare: a variety of Allied tanks entrained at Tank Corps Central Stores, Erin, near St Pol, 1918. On the left, British Whippet light tanks, in the centre British Mark V heavy tanks, and on the right French Renault light tanks.**
(TM 890/F2)

himself fighting a defensive action where, only a few months before, he had been pushing back the Germans. The line broke at Laventie, 11 miles (18km) west of Lille, where a weak Portuguese unit was unable to take the strain, and the action developed to the north-west as they and the British fell back to Estaires on the Lys. On the southern flank of the gap the 55th Division held firm, and the German intrusion spread northwards towards the southern edge of the Ypres Salient.

On 11 April Armentières was evacuated and Haig issued his famous appeal to his men "…to fight it out! Every position must be held to the last man: there must be no retirement. With our backs to the wall … each one of us must fight on to the end." The Germans were at Ploegsteert Wood the next day, and took Messines, Wytschaete and St

Eloi. The thrust to Dunkirk was, however, slackening by the time the Germans were approaching Hazebrouck, and there the British held them. An optimistic Kaiser arrived in Armentières to take part in what he expected to be a victorious advance. He was to be disappointed yet again.

At Bailleul on 13 April the 34th and 59th Divisions withstood the German attack, yielding only half a mile of ground, and fighting continued on the Messines Ridge where the ANZACs defended and counter-attacked with stubborn courage. The bloodily won ridge of Passchendaele was evacuated on 15 April and Plumer withdrew his five divisions to a line around Ypres approximating to that of 1915. The British divisions were below complement and the new men – the

replacements for the losses of Third Ypres – were young and incompletely trained, though they fought bravely. Pétain, the French Commander-in-Chief, had, however, managed to move five French divisions to strengthen the sector. The Germans then turned their efforts to securing the high ground south of the town, the line of hills from Mount Kemmel, through Mont Noir to the Mont des Cats. The French 28th Division held Mount Kemmel and the 154th were at Dranoutre to the south-east. A massive German gas bombardment of the Ypres line took place on 20 April and on 25 April, at 3.30am, another gas bombardment was concentrated on the French. Seven German divisions moved forward with heavy artillery support. The British fell back to Dickebusch Lake to the north of the French who were taking the major force of the attack. The French 30th Regiment was wiped out and when the 99th attempted to counter-attack they were attacked in their turn. The Germans infiltrated to the west of the objective and the surviving French fell back on Locre. Here the line held, while the British to the north also held their positions. The attack was renewed on 29 April by 13 German divisions. It failed, and with it the Second Battle of the Lys was over. The losses had been heavy: 76,300 British and 35,000 French. But the Germans had suffered 109,300 casualties, and, worse, failed to break through to the coast.

Ludendorff remained certain that victory could be achieved in Flanders, but with the French presence the Allied line there proved too tough a nut to crack. Once more, therefore, as at Verdun, he would launch an attack the French could not fail to oppose with all their strength and thus weaken the approaches to the Channel. He struck towards Paris by way of the Aisne and the Marne in June. Again the effort came within a hairbreadth of success, but here the Germans met the Americans in force for the first time, and at Château-Thierry and Belleau Wood they proved their worth.

From then on the tide flowed consistently in the Allies' favour. At Hamel, on 4 July, an Australian

Above **French soldiers and a British sergeant with a Renault tank. Although comparatively fast, the Renaults were limited by being undermanned; they had a crew of two. The driver was fully employed with his task, leaving the commander to serve as lookout and gunner as well as directing the tank. Although flawed, this arrangement did work when the tanks were used in large numbers, over good ground and against clearly defined targets.** (TM 890/D2)

The creeping bombardment was followed by a tank advance with infantry support.

force, with a small American detachment, under Lieutenant-General Sir John Monash gave a demonstration of how the war could be fought. A combined operation involving artillery, tanks, infantry and aircraft nipped out a salient in 93 minutes. The creeping bombardment was followed by a tank advance with infantry support to occupy the ground. Heavy loads for the infantry were avoided: they carried only their immediate requirements and were resupplied with machine-gun ammunition by air. The Battle of Amiens in

August built on this approach, leap frogging the artillery forward as the advance progressed so that the infantry were never unsupported. Rather than risk outrunning their lines of supply, the Australians and Canadians resisted the temptation to charge on after a remarkable eight-mile advance. By September they were ready to smash the Hindenburg Line.

South of the Ypres Salient the Allies had been hacking away at the German positions at the tip of the ground gained in the Battle of the Lys, and by 1 September the line south of Armentières was all but regained. On 4 September the British were back at Ploegsteert. The Fourth Battle of Ypres opened on 28 September. The Allied Flanders Army Group consisted of 12 Belgian divisions, under King Albert and General Degoutte, in the northern sector, and 10 British and six French, which stood broadly where the Allies had started in June 1917. In his diary Brigadier-General J. L. Jack, commanding 28 Brigade, wrote:

How familiar the place-names of today were 14 months ago ... The bones of most of my officers and many of the other ranks lie between here and Zonnebeke.

The Belgians swept forward through the Houthulst Forest and on to Passchendaele on that first day. The British regained Wytschaete. The advance was four and a half miles at the least, and in some places as much as six miles. On 29 September they leapt forward as far again, but rain, as usual, was making the going difficult, particularly

Above left **French uniforms of 1918. From left: private of the Artillerie Spéciale, that is, the tanks; private, 177th Regiment of Artillery; private, Regiment of Colonial Infantry of Morocco.** (Osprey, MAA 286, *French Army 1914-1918*) (Gerry Embleton)

Below left **The German High Command was shocked by the lack of discipline shown by a significant proportion of their troops in the advances of March to July 1918, indicative of a fatal decline in morale. The troops who have taken this British 18-pounder battery show small inclination to join their comrades, seen hauling their cut-down Russian 7.62cm Infanterie-Geschütz (close-support weapon) in the distance.** (Osprey, MAA 80, *German Army 1914-18*) (Gerry Embleton)

in keeping the forward troops supplied. On 2 October the situation became severe; French and British troops had run out of food. Eighty aircraft were used to drop 15,000 rations to them, small sacks containing five or ten packs padded with earth to break their fall when slung out of the aeroplane. This first drop of rations to troops in the field constituted a load of 13 tons. The ravaged countryside was clearly an obstacle to further progress and the battle ceased the same day with the British just two miles short of Menin – their objective in the distant autumn of 1914. The British had lost 4,695 killed and wounded, the Belgians 4,500. Between them they had taken over 10,000 Germans prisoner, 300 guns and 600 machine-guns. In the Ypres Salient the war was almost over.

On 14 October the last shell fell on the rub-ble that had been Ypres. It was said that a man on horseback could see clear across the town. On 16 October it became possible to travel, with difficulty, over the ruined road, all the way to Menin. As the Germans were driven back in Belgium, on the Sambre and in the Argonne, and as mutiny and civil unrest swept Germany itself, a Germany nearing starvation from the effects of the Allied blockade, frantic negotiations for an armistice were conducted. On 11 November, at 11am, the fighting on the Western Front came to an end.

Above left **The French fought stubbornly to resist German conquest of Mount Kemmel, and continued to do so after they were pushed off. Their dead now rest in the ossuary on the slopes of the hill.** (MFME Yp/Ar 2/7)

Above **A solution to mobility for artillery, the gun carrier *Darlington*, a tank modified to carry a 6-inch artillery piece. The gun's wheels are slung on the sides of the tank. 1918.** (TM 883/A6)

Left **German troops on Mount Kemmel, May 1918.** (IWM Q.47999 – German Official)

BIBLIOGRAPHY

The literature of the First World War is immense and that of the various battles fought in the Ypres Salient substantial. The list given here is of those works the author has consulted most often in writing this book, and is therefore partial and personal. The books from which quotations are taken are included.

Adam-Smith, Patsy, *The ANZACs,* Melbourne, Thomas Nelson, 1978.

Anon., *Ieper en de Frontstreek, Sint-Niklaas,* A. G. Claus, undated.

Anon., *Ypres and the Battles for Ypres,* Michelin Guides, 1920, reissued London, Naval and Military Press, undated.

Ashurst, George, ed. Richard Holmes, *My Bit,* Marlborough, Crowood Press, 1987.

Banks, Arthur, *A Military Atlas of the First World War,* London, Leo Cooper, 1975; 1989.

Bernard, H., *Guerre Totale et Guerre Révolutionaire,* 1977.

Brown, Malcolm, and Shirley Seaton, *Christmas Truce,* London, Leo Cooper/Secker & Warburg, 1984; Papermac, 1994.

Browne, D. G., *The Tank in Action,* Edinburgh and London, William Blackwood, 1920.

Chappell, Mike, Elite 61, *The Guards Divisions 1914-18,* London, Osprey, 1995.

Chappell, Mike, Men-at-Arms 182, *British Battle Insignia 1 1914-18,* London, Osprey, 1986

Coombs, Rose E. B., revised Karel Margry, *Before*

Endeavours Fade, London, After the Battle, 1994.

Dunstan, Simon, Men-at-Arms 157, *Flak Jackets,* London, Osprey, 1984.

Fosten D.S.V., & R.J. Marrion, Men-at-Arms 80, *The German Army 1914-18,* London, Osprey, 1978.

Gilbert, Martin, *First World War,* London, Weidenfeld & Nicolson, 1994.

Giles, John, *Flanders Then and Now,* London, Leo Cooper; 1970, Battle of Britain Prints International, 1987.

Glover, Michael, *A New Guide to the Battlefields of Northern France and the Low Countries,* London, Michael Joseph, 1987.

Gray, Randal, with Christopher Argyle, *Chronicle of the First World War, Vols I & II,* Oxford & New York, Facts on File, 1990 & 1991.

Griffiths, William R., *The Great War,* West Point Military History Series, Wayne, NJ, Avery, 1986.

Holt, Tonie and Valmai, *Battlefields of the First World War,* London, Pavilion, 1993.

Holt, Tonie and Valmai, *The Ypres Salient,* London, Leo Cooper/Secker & Warburg, undated.

Johnson, Hubert C., *Breakthrough!,* Novato, Calif., Presidio, 1994.

Liddell Hart, Basil, *The War in Outline, 1914-1918,* London, Faber and Faber, 1936.

Livesey, Anthony, *The Viking Atlas of World War I,* London, Viking/Penguin, 1994.

McCarthy, Chris, *The Third Ypres: Passchendaele; The Day-by-Day Account,* London, Arms and Armour, 1995.

Macdonald, Lyn, *1914 – The Days of Hope,* London, Michael Joseph, 1987; Penguin Books, 1989.

Macdonald, Lyn, *1915 – The Death of Innocence,* London, Headline, 1993.

Macdonald, Lyn, *They Called it Passchendaele,* London, Michael Joseph, 1978; Penguin Books, 1993.

Marix Evans, Martin, *Ypres in War and Peace,* Andover, Pitkin, 1992.

Nicholson, G. W. L., *Canadian Expeditionary Force 1914-1918,* Ottawa, Queen's Printer, 1962.

Parker, Ernest, *Into Battle 1914-1918,* London, Longmans, Green, 1964; Leo Cooper, 1994.

Pegler, Martin, Warrior 16, *British Tommy 1914-18,* London, Osprey, 1996.

Shermer, *David, La Grande Guerre 1914-1918,* Paris, 1973.

Spagnoly, Tony, *The Anatomy of a Raid,* London, Multidream Publications, 1991.

Swinton, E. D. and the Earl Percy, *A Year Ago,* London, Edward Arnold, 1916.

Terraine, John, *To Win a War: 1918, The Year of Victory,* London, Macmillan, 1986.

Tuchman, Barbara W., *August 1914,* London, Constable, 1962.

Vaughan, Edwin Campion, *Some Desperate Glory,* London, Frederick Warne, 1981.

Wolff, Leon, *In Flanders Fields,* London, Longmans, Green, 1959.

Westlake, Ray, Men-at-Arms 245, *British Territorial Units,* London, Osprey, 1991.

INDEX

'Their Name Liveth
For Evermore'

Lille Gate Cemetery, Ypres